P9-DCM-290

THE DISNEY WAY

THE DISNEY WAY

Harnessing the Management Secrets of Disney in Your Company

Bill Capodagli

Lynn Jackson

McGraw-Hill
New York   Chicago   San Francisco   Lisbon   London   Madrid
Mexico City   Milan   New Delhi   San Juan   Seoul
Singapore   Sydney   Toronto

The McGraw·Hill Companies

Library of Congress Cataloging-in-Publication Data

Capodagli, Bill.
   The Disney way / harnessing the management secrets of Disney in your company / Bill Capodagli, Lynn Jackson.
      p.   cm.
   Includes index.
   ISBN 0-07-012064-1
   1. Walt Disney Company—Management.   I. Jackson, Lynn.
II. Title.
PN1999.W27C37   1998
384'.8'0979494—dc21   98-42938
                                                                        CIP

Copyright © 2002 by Center for Quality Leadership. All rights reserved. Printed in the United States of America. Except as permitted under the United States Copyright Act of 1976, no part of this publication may be reproduced or distributed in any form or by any means, or stored in a data base or retrieval system, without the prior written permission of the publisher.

Walt Disney Company Trademarks: *The Disney Way* is in no way authorized by, endorsed, or affiliated with The Walt Disney Company, Inc., or Walt Disney World. The Disney trademarks include but are not limited to The Magic Kingdom, Adventureland, Animal Kingdom, Disneyland Paris, and Walt Disney. All references to such trademarked properties are used in accordance with the Fair Use Doctrine and are not meant to imply that this book is a Disney product for advertising or other commercial purposes.

          9 10 11 12   FGR/FGR   0 5 4   (HC)
    6 7 8 9 10 11 12   FGR/FGR   0 5 4   (PBK)

ISBN 0-07-012064-1 (HC)
ISBN 0-07-137969-X (PBK)

The editing supervisor was Jane Palmieri, and the production supervisor was Sherri Souffrance. It was set in Fairfield per the NBF specs by Michele Zito and Paul Scozzari of McGraw-Hill's Professional Book Group composition unit, Hightstown, N.J.

Printed and bound by Quebecor/Fairfield.

McGraw-Hill books are available at special quantity discounts to use as premiums and sales promotions, or for use in corporate training programs. For more information, please write to the Director of Special Sales, McGraw-Hill Professional, Two Penn Plaza, New York, NY 10121-2298. Or contact your local bookstore.

To Bob Stallings: Whose great courage inspired us to continue our life's work, even in the face of deep tragedy.

CONTENTS

FOREWORD

"How *do* they do it?" As a kid, that's what haunted me when I was dazzled by great magicians. Wouldn't it be great if I could do that? The same question, "How *do* they do it?" popped up in my mind when I reflected on Disney's performance.

For Disney is awesome. It's the longest running show on earth. For 75 years, its fantasies and larger-than-life experiences have swept away kids and adults of all ages, producing one winner after another, never looking tired or out of date. That's no mean feat when you consider that Disney's business requires a steady stream of new ideas and constant reinvention of the product. When you're only as good as your last film or your last theme park attraction, there isn't much room for either artistic or financial flops.

And think about the company's amazing brand. I would be hard-pressed to come up with more than a handful of remote locales where the name Walt Disney doesn't evoke at least minimal recognition. If not the Disney name, then certainly the Disney characters are bound to bring a knowing smile to faces of children and adults from Burbank to Beijing, Honolulu to Helsinki. So I kept asking myself, how *do* they do it? How do these people perpetuate their magic? Don't they ever run out of ideas? How do they continue to dazzle customers—their "guests"—all over the world with characters that Walt Disney dreamed up when our grandparents were kids?

As I discovered by reading this book, there's more to Disney's tale of greatness than abundant creativity, hard work, and that never-say-die spirit.

What were Walt Disney's values and vision, and what role did they play in the company's amazing achievements?

The Disney success has as much to do with Walt's suresighted management principles as with his entertainment and business savvy. From the hiring and training of employees to the realization of a creative concept and the company's exceptional focus on customer service—everything is linked to Walt's values and beliefs. Few people are aware of the master's guiding principles, and even fewer realize how those principles can be applied to organizations far removed from Hollywood, whether chemical businesses in Louisiana or software makers in Oregon.

In *The Disney Way*, Bill Capodagli and Lynn Jackson take you on a fascinating trip through the wonderful world of Disney, both yesterday and today. The company's model of management remains as fresh and effective today as it was at its inception 75 years ago. A lot has changed in those 75 years: The technology is more sophisticated, the attractions at the theme parks more exciting, and the musicals more spectacular. But Michael Eisner and his Dream Team who run the Disney "show" today still rely on the sound management principles that Walt Disney himself built into his company more than seven decades ago.

And as Bill and Lynn's string of successful clients attests, those principles of good management that form the "Disney way" can work their magic on any organization, including yours.

Fred Wiersema
Business strategist and coauthor
of The Discipline of Market Leaders

PREFACE TO THE PAPERBACK EDITION

With the release of the hardcover edition of *The Disney Way* in December 1998, we knew we had something special. *Fortune* was our first reviewer, selecting *The Disney Way* as one of their "Best Business Books of 1999" and touting it as "so useful you may whistle while you work."

But as time goes on, we are more and more delighted to learn of the numerous organizations that have embraced *The Disney Way*. Arguably the highest praise of *The Disney Way* comes directly from Disney cast members. *BusinessWeek* wrote a report about what the big companies were reading, and *The Disney Way* captured the #3 spot right behind CEO Michael Eisner's book, *Work in Progress*.

The true test of the book's usefulness, however, is in the trenches—in the companies trying to adopt a *Disney Way* culture of Dream, Believe, Dare, Do. Once thought to be a success credo that worked only for Walt Disney, it is indeed working in places far removed from the entertainment industry: in dentistry, in banks, in retail, in state government, and beyond!

You may ask, "How can our organization do what Disney does? We don't have their cast members, their operations, or their world recognition." Now, of course, we understand how frightening changing one's culture can be. We believe the fear is twofold: one, it's CHANGE, and, two, companies don't know where to begin. No one we know of besides Mickey Mouse and Tinker Bell can wave a magic wand and inspire people. That is not our mission. Through the principles outlined in this book, we stress the importance of attaining a Disney-esque culture of customer intimacy, creativity, and teamwork that is essential in today's volatile business marketplace.

As we write in our book *Leading at the Speed of Change: Using New Economy Rules to Invigorate Old Economy*

Companies, "Culture is the key to success.... it must be disseminated and reinforced—over and over and over—until it is absorbed throughout the ranks." No one is immune from this guiding principle of success. And the Dream, Believe, Dare, Do culture is one that has proven to achieve results. Some companies use our *Disney Way Fieldbook* to infuse this culture into their own; some ask us for consultation and support. The key is making it stick by doing whatever it takes.

Once you have experienced the sheer awe of the setting, the service, and the systems at a Disney theme park, you will *know* this is the type of culture your company will want and will need, and the one that will have others wishing for the secret to your success.

And lastly, we want to thank those who have Dared to Dream, have stayed the course, and who are doing business as "show" business!

PREFACE

Mickey Mouse management isn't a joke. It's the ticket to your business future.

Everyone knows that success in today's business world comes from inspired creativity and disciplined teamwork. *And* everyone knows that The Walt Disney Company is the master of both.

But how did the company weave itself into the very fabric of our society? How did it create the legacy that still endures some 30 years after the death of its legendary founder? What were the rock-solid principles upon which Walt Disney built his namesake?

This book tells the inside story of just how Disney's success was achieved—not by epiphanic flashes of creative insight that produced a *Pinocchio* or a *Dumbo*, but by the force of a much-considered, carefully wrought process of managing innovation and creativity and by adherence to a firmly held system of beliefs.

The principles and techniques that underlie that system, as articulated by Walt Disney himself, can be applied to companies everywhere. For example, it was Walt Disney who pioneered and perfected the use of storyboards as idea-generation, project-management, and problem-solving tools. And it was Walt Disney who created his own "university" solely for the purpose of training employees.

The Disney way breaks the intellectual framework to allow companies to soar beyond the limits of traditional management. For entry-level recruits and CEOs, for private companies and public agencies, the Disney principles are redefining the nature of business in our age and revolutionizing the art of management.

ACKNOWLEDGMENTS

The passion that we have for the Disney organization is a direct result of the passion that Walt and Roy Disney had for their company from the beginning . . . the dream of something great to be created through hard work and perseverance.

Neither one of us visited Disneyland or Disney World as children. But we both have been fortunate to experience the park through the eyes of the children in our families. Our heartfelt thanks to Bill's children, Billy, Alan, Susan, and Tony Capodagli, and Lynn's niece, Jaimie Brougham. A special thanks to Alan, Bill's mentally handicapped son. Alan is our perpetual five-year-old, and he allows us to experience the magic of the Disney theme parks through his innocence and wide-eyed wonder.

Our dream of writing this book would not have materialized without the editorial genius of Donna Carpenter and her team at Wordworks. Many thanks to Maurice Coyle for his creative input and to Martha Lawler for her great attention to detail and for keeping us on track.

A special thanks to our editor at McGraw-Hill, Mary Glenn, whose enthusiasm for this project made it all worth it, and, of course, to Helen Rees, our agent, for her persistence and support.

This book would have been just another Disney book without the examples from the wonderful companies we have been privileged to work with over the years. We are especially thankful for the opportunity to work with Whirlpool's Evansville Global Technology Center, under the extraordinarily competent leadership of Steve Paddock. Also, a special thanks to Jerry McColgin, leader of Whirlpool's Global No-Frost Team, for his input on the book and for allowing us to be part of, as Jerry says, "a whacko group of people from around the world, who clearly weren't going to fit into a conventional business mold."

Many thanks to Dr. Bill Cross, Vice President at Mead Johnson Nutritional Division of Bristol-Myers Squibb in Evansville, Indiana, for his commitment to the process of cultural transformation.

We wish to honor Ken Blanchard, who demonstrated his belief in the Disney way concept by authoring a powerful endorsement for us. We also sincerely appreciate Fred Wiersema for taking the time out of his busy schedule to write the foreword. A warm thanks to our fellow Disney admirers, Bette Davis and Dr. Ken Davis, for their editorial consultation and encouragement on this project.

A huge round of applause to JoAnne Sebree, our no-nonsense administrative assistant, who created all those great "mechanisms" to keep us sane during this long process.

A personal thank you to Father Carl Deitchman, John Wilson, and all the fine people at St. Meinrad Archabbey in St. Meinrad, Indiana, for their prayers and patience during our recovery from the C130 plane crash in Evansville, Indiana, on February 6, 1992.

We are eternally indebted to Bob Stallings for his encouragement and support in our recovery from the C130 plane crash in Evansville in February of 1992. After the trauma of losing his son, John, in this tragedy and a third of his workforce, Bob continued to serve as a role model of strength, loyalty, and integrity in leadership to us. Bob gave Bill some of the best advice in his hospital room, which was to "get back to work as soon as possible." And for both of us, doing what we love turned out to be the greatest healer of all. We are also thankful for all the members of the Plumbing and Industrial Supply family who not only supported us during our recovery but also miraculously rebuilt their company to the level of great success it can claim today.

Bill Capodagli
Lynn Jackson

WALT'S WAY

My only hope is that we never lose sight of one thing...that it all started with a mouse.

WALT DISNEY, 1954

When a young midwestern artist was struggling to get his first filmmaking business off the ground in 1923, he borrowed $500 from an uncle. The uncle insisted on repayment in cash rather than taking an ownership interest in the venture. That young artist, Walter Elias Disney, went on to advance the demanding art of animation to new heights and founded a company based on such sound business principles that it has survived for nearly three-quarters of a century and has influenced virtually every aspect of American culture.

Hindsight, of course, has a well-deserved reputation for startling clarity, and we don't know if the uncle lived long enough to feel a full measure of regret. But had he opted for stock in the Disney Company instead of a cash repayment, the return on his $500 would have amounted to almost a *billion* dollars from 1923 to the present.

How did a boy born into rather modest circumstances in turn-of-the-century Chicago accomplish so much? Legend has it that Walt Disney explained his success this way: "I dream, I test my dreams against my beliefs, I dare to take risks, and I execute my vision to make those dreams come true."

Dream, Believe, Dare, Do: These words reverberate across the decades of Disney achievement. Everything Walt did— every choice he made, every strategy he pursued—evolved

1

from these four concepts. And as the bedrock upon which his life and work rested, they naturally informed the basic values that dictated how he ran his company. Thus, the ways in which the Walt Disney Company trained and empowered its employees, managed creativity and innovation, and provided service to its customers all were influenced by this four-pillared philosophy.

WHY DISNEY?

The more we learn about this legendary figure and his achievements, both as an artist and as a creative business leader, the more certain it becomes that the Disney story embodies valuable lessons for every company. But most of us were originally drawn to Walt Disney and the company he founded as one is drawn to a favorite uncle.

Like nearly everyone else alive today, we, the authors, grew up being almost as familiar with the Disney name as we were with our own. Many childhood hours were spent sitting on the floor before the TV set watching *The Wonderful World of Disney* and being transported to the Magic Kingdom. Nor has either of us forgotten the thrill of seeing *Peter Pan* for the first time.

As a young father introducing my own children to the film, I [Bill] marveled at its ability to rekindle the emotions I had initially felt as a six-year-old. Disneyland, too, had much the same effect the first time I visited some 25 years ago. Not surprisingly, my then three-year-old son didn't want to leave, and, I might add, I felt a little bit that way myself.

In this instance, though, I was captivated by much more than the fabulous attractions. Viewing the park through the eyes of an industrial engineer, I was thoroughly intrigued by the processes. How did the Disney people manage all those crowds? How did they train their employees? How did they run their customer service? What was the secret of the success of their complex technology? I came away from that first visit deeply impressed by the organization—and with a lot of questions.

As for me [Lynn], *The Wonderful World of Disney* was one of the best things about being a child. Later, when I became heavily involved in the field of training and development, I realized the true magic of Disney's philosophy. For me, the seed for benchmarking Disney was planted when I took a copy of *Service America* with me on a trip to Florida in the mid-eighties. I knew it would help prepare me to conduct an upcoming seminar for a group of salespeople from all over the country. Reading Albrecht and Zemke's book, I had one of those experiences when a light goes on in your head: Walt Disney insisted that every employee *is* the company in the mind of the customer. From that point on, my goal in training salespeople became to inspire them to begin living that mindset. Then, on my next trip to Disney World, I closely observed the best of the best in action, doing just that.

Years later, when we started looking around for companies that could serve as examples in our consulting business, we found ourselves coming back again and again to Disney. A great deal of scrutinizing, analyzing, and researching of various companies led us to conclude that none compared to Disney in every aspect of running an organization. Whereas one company might excel in customer relations or another might work well with its suppliers, Disney's consistency in direction and overall strategy, its unrivaled customer service, its employee training and related low turnover, its product creativity, and its spectacular profitability combined, in our view, to make it the perfect business model.

Having studied the Disney phenomenon for 20 years, we are convinced that the management techniques we call "Walt's way" are as valid today as they were in 1937, when the classic *Snow White and the Seven Dwarfs,* the very first animated feature film, captured the hearts of moviegoers. Skeptics need only look to the spectacular successes the Disney Company continues to achieve year after year, decade after decade, for affirmation of Walt's way.

And if you're wondering whether the Disney magic has legs, we can answer with a resounding yes! Over the years, we have encouraged clients in many different industries to use

Walt's fundamental credo to improve their customer service, productivity, and internal operations, while at the same time creating an atmosphere of fun. The company that Disney founded has, in effect, served as a laboratory for us and, in turn, our clients.

This chapter introduces the ten principles at the heart of the Disney legend. Subsequent chapters then take up these principles in detail and show how they are still being lived at the company today and how some of our clients have adapted them to fit their specific circumstances, enabling them to create winning solutions. Their success stories attest to the continuing power of Walt's way.

BENCHMARKING A LEGEND

Like many other young men of his time and place, Walt Disney held a succession of jobs punctuated by stints of formal education. His skill as an artist and his interest in cartoons took him to California in 1923, and only four years later he formed Walt Disney Productions. Disney's first big success came the following year, in 1928, when he introduced the character of Mickey Mouse in the synchronized sound cartoon *Steamboat Willie*. The cartoon and the mouse were an instant hit.

By the 1930s, this endearing little scamp had captured the hearts of audiences worldwide. Known as Michael Maus in Germany, Miki Kuchi in Japan, and Miguel Ratonocito in Spain, he even had a car named after him! When Fiat, the Italian automobile company, produced its first small car shortly after World War II, it was christened *Topolino*, Mickey's Italian nickname. Even though Mickey became a senior citizen a few years back, his ageless persona continues to be recognized and loved by young and old on every continent.

Mickey may have led the parade, but Disney was not a one-mouse band by a long shot. No other company in the notoriously chancy entertainment business has ever achieved the stability, phenomenal growth, and multidirectional expansion of Disney.

In spite of its ever-increasing reach, however, the Disney Company has consistently kept to the central course described by its founder at the outset: to provide the finest in family entertainment. Firmly grounded in Walt's innate sense of principle and his midwestern values, this mission has, over the years, become clearly associated with the Disney brand. Audiences expect it, and they are seldom disappointed.

Whatever form the entertainment might take—a theme park ride, a Broadway musical, an Ice Capades production— it has to be a good show in every regard. When Walt talked about delivering "the good show," he didn't mean simply a glittering spectacle relying on superficial bells and whistles. He meant an entirely original, perfectly executed production with substance, one created to delight a wide audience. He believed that this was what customers wanted and expected from him, and he was fanatical about providing it.

What's more, the concept of a good show encompasses far more than the on-stage action in a single production. Because Disney insisted that customers be treated like guests, great customer service has become a standard feature of the total package the Disney Company offers. And wrapped up in that package is a gift of creativity—in product, service, and process—that makes even jaded adults smile with child-like delight.

Accomplishing such magic obviously requires the contributions and assistance of a talented, dedicated, and loyal staff as well as an army of suppliers and other partners. Extensive training, constant reinforcement of the Disney culture and its values, and recognition of the valuable contributions that employees and partners make combine to keep people turning out one fantastic show after another as they strive to meet the exacting standards Walt established.

It is this consistency of direction, obsession with customer service, commitment to people, and creative excellence that make the Disney Company a standard by which others might be judged and an exemplary enterprise from which others can learn.

A CONSUMMATE DREAMER

Walt Disney was so successful as a businessman that people are often startled to learn that he was a lifelong dreamer who started out as a commercial artist. But it was precisely his unfettered imagination, coupled with a bent for experimentation, that propelled him to the pinnacle of success. Far from being a hindrance, dreaming was the wellspring of Disney's creativity.

The story is told that as a schoolboy in art class, Walt was assigned to draw flowers. In what might now be seen as a quintessential touch, and, indeed, the precursor to many of Disney's animated characters, young Walt embellished his work by sketching a face in the center of each flower. His teacher was less than impressed by the boy's deviation from the norm, and lacking a mirror like the one the wicked queen had in *Snow White,* failed to recognize the creative genius whose dream world would make him one of the most famous artists in history.

Perhaps because he himself was the greatest of dreamers, Walt encouraged both his artisans and his hundreds of other employees to unleash their imaginations too. He knew that a reservoir of creative power often languishes within a company's ranks simply because no one ever bothers to tap it. Rather than hire someone for one specific purpose and forever pigeonhole that person—as is the norm at too many companies—Disney not only welcomed ideas from all of his employees, he actively sought to turn them into reality.

From dreams spring ideas, and from ideas comes innovation, the lifeblood of any company. Walt Disney instinctively knew, however, that an unshakable belief—in one's principles, in one's associates and employees, and in customers—is necessary before ideas can successfully evolve into innovation.

No matter how ingenious an idea was, no matter what kind of financial interests were at stake, Disney demanded that the company adhere to his belief in and commitment to honesty, reliability, loyalty, and respect for people as individuals. Whether he was producing a cartoon or building an amusement park, he refused to palm off a shoddy product on his audience.

When *Pinocchio* was released in February 1940, *The New York Times* hailed it as "the best cartoon ever made." But *Pinocchio* had a difficult birth. The story of the puppet-maker Geppetto and his "son" Pinocchio, the all-but-human puppet he created, was six months into production, and the team of animation artists was almost halfway through its meticulous, time-consuming drawings for the full-length feature when Walt Disney called a halt. Pinocchio was altogether *too* wooden, he said, and the character proposed for Jiminy Cricket made him look too much like, well, a cricket. Never mind that $500,000 had already been spent, Disney was not deterred. Previous efforts were tossed aside, and Disney called Ward Kimball, one of his talented young animators, into his office.

Kimball, who was upset because his labors on *Snow White* had ended up on the cutting-room floor, was planning to use the occasion to resign when Disney summoned him. But the animator never had a chance. He got so excited listening to Disney talk about his dreams for the film and his ideas about Jiminy Cricket that Kimball entirely forgot his own intentions of resigning. Instead, he stayed at the company and went on to create a cricket that was more human than insect, one that embodied the spirit of hope which children of all ages possess but which sometimes needs reinforcing.

The decision to halt the production of *Pinocchio* was made because the movie was failing to live up to one of Walt Disney's principles, his insistence on excellence. At the time, Disney already had won worldwide acclaim. He probably could have let the film go as it was without doing any serious damage to his company or his reputation—and with substantial savings. But Disney recognized the difference between adequate and excellent, and he would not compromise.

That's not to say that Disney was a spendthrift. Quite the contrary: He was always acutely aware of the bottom line; he simply refused to let it dictate every decision he made. "Why should we let a few dollars jeopardize our chances?" Walt once wrote to his brother Roy.[1] Before it was finished, *Pinocchio* cost $3 million, more than any other animated picture up to that point. Although high-priced for its day, this film classic long ago paid for itself in the degree of sophisticated animation, craftsmanship, and artwork it achieves.

Disney's strength as an imaginative and principled creative force grew from his willingness to take risks, to experiment, and to invest his resources and his time in new ventures. From the beginning, he searched for innovative ways to give his audiences the best of all possible entertainment fare. He pioneered a new art form in making *Snow White*, and he did it in the face of nearly unanimous ridicule.

"No one will sit through a 90-minute cartoon," people told him. But Disney ignored the naysayers and clung tenaciously to his dream, confident that he could produce a film that would appeal to both adults and children. His willingness to buck accepted wisdom and take a risk paid handsome dividends: *Snow White and the Seven Dwarfs*, which was released in 1937, grossed $8 million, an astonishing amount when you consider that at the time movie tickets cost only pennies. It received a special Academy Award, and some consider it to be one of the greatest films ever made. *Snow White* has also been equally popular in reissue, with a box office take that places it in the top 50 all-time highest-grossing films.

In just a dozen years, roughly 1930 to 1942, Walt Disney managed to transform animation from a marginal segment of the entertainment industry to a new art form. He used technical innovations to create a seamless mixture of story, color, and sound. Knowing that great visions require great, but calculated, risks, Disney dared to follow his instincts.

Among our own clients, we have seen how a willingness to go beyond the ordinary, to take personal risks can bring great rewards too. At a seminar we conducted for Whirlpool, for example, we encountered a young woman, Debbie, who had been asked to join a high-risk, high-profile team. The promotion meant a big step up in responsibility and promised good prospects for the future, but she hesitated for fear of losing the safety and security of her current job.

"I'm afraid," Debbie confessed to us, so we spoke with her about the need to take a long-term view of her situation, to weigh the risks against the opportunities the way Walt Disney would have done. We also encouraged her to recognize that the project was vital to the company and that it was a testimony to her talents to be asked to join this team.

As a result, Debbie worked through her concerns, took the risk, and because of her accomplishments as a committed team member, went on to earn further assignments and promotions.

TURNING DREAMS INTO REALITY

Walt Disney's stellar accomplishments might suggest that he had no difficulty in taking whatever action was needed to bring his dreams to fulfillment. It was not always easy, however, particularly when a lot of skeptics stood in the way, but Disney knew that dreams are sterile things unless the dreamer can do what it takes to make them come true.

When his fertile mind produced an idea, he set about transforming that idea into a concrete product, service, or process. If his methods of executing his vision were sometimes unconventional or broke the accepted rules, so be it. The point was to put on the good show.

For example, when Disneyland was being built in the early 1950s, Walt himself was often on site checking every detail. He spent countless hours with the creative and knowledgeable staff he had hired, putting his personal stamp on everything from landscape design to attractions to music.

But then he did something rather unusual: He asked everyone who was working on Disneyland, from electricians to executives, to test each ride as it was completed. There was nothing new about Disney's reaching for perfection, but the park was on a tight schedule with opening day near at hand, and this idea clearly seemed to be a waste of time and money. Imagine asking your janitors, elevator operators, or other low-level employees for critical input about a new product or service just before you're ready to launch it. Disney's request was a bit far-fetched. Or was it?

Although a great deal of what Disney did sounds strange to many managers, this was Walt's way of doing whatever needed to be done to achieve his vision. It was another way of making absolutely sure that everything was the best that it could be and that nothing was missing.

As it turned out, something *was* missing from a swashbuckling Disneyland attraction called "The Pirates of the Caribbean." A construction worker, or "cast member" in Disney's language, who happened to hail from Louisiana bayou country, approached the boss after taking the ride and told him, "Something's missing, but I can't figure out what it is."

"Ride it again and keep on riding until you've figured it out," Walt told him.

Finally, after repeated trips through Disney's Caribbean, the cast member realized what was wrong: In tropical climates, the night should be alive with fireflies, but there were none on this attraction. In short order, Walt Disney saw to it that his version of a Caribbean fantasy had fireflies blinking in the dark.

Whether it was fireflies in a theme park attraction, the portrayal of a wise and lovable cricket, the treatment of a Disney "guest," or the removal of a candy wrapper threatening to litter Disneyland's landscape, Walt was a perfectionist down to the last detail. As for those candy wrappers, it isn't only the staff of street cleaners that is charged with litter removal at Disney parks. *Any* employee who spots a bit of trash sweeps it up practically before it flutters to the ground. That is part of the Disney culture that is ingrained in everyone from the beginning. Employees of the Disney Company are trained extensively, and the Disney mindset is constantly reinforced because Walt considered such an approach essential to executing his vision.

He also knew that execution was impossible without a framework within which ideas could be effectively implemented while controlling costs. To that end, the company follows a rigorous process of project management. And to solve problems that arrive in planning and communicating project ideas, it has adapted the storyboarding technique originally used to keep track of the thousands of drawings needed for animation of cartoon features.

Execution of ideas is never left to chance in the Disney universe. It is a well-planned process.

EMBRACING THE DISNEY SPIRIT

Dream. Believe. Dare. Do. Just as Walt Disney never wavered from his four-pillared philosophy, history is replete with examples of great accomplishments derived from the same commitment. We are reminded, for example, of President John F. Kennedy's challenge to America in 1961 to put the first man on the moon in the ensuing decade. Kennedy had a dream that he firmly believed could become a reality because he saw that it fit perfectly with the can-do spirit that has driven the United States from its outset. To make such a commitment and to embark on this monumental space project was daring, to be sure. But in the doing, America not only saw a man set foot on the moon's surface, it reaped scientific benefits of far-reaching significance for the entire world (Fig. 1-1).

So, too, have the principles that Walt Disney espoused led to unimagined glories as the empire he established continues to grow and thrive. Back in 1923, it's doubtful that even Walt

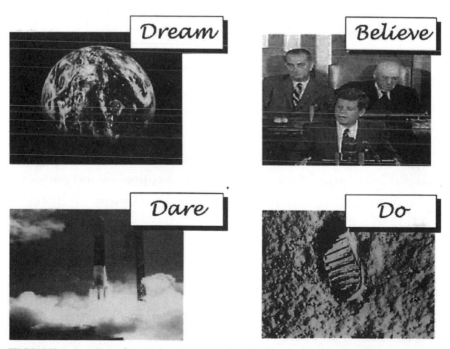

FIGURE 1-1.   President John F. Kennedy's challenge to America in 1961 to put the first man on the moon.

himself could have foreseen that the Disney interests would one day extend to movies, television, Broadway theater, amusement parks, an ice hockey team, and a vacation club (not to mention the nation's largest laundry facility at Disney World).

Disneyland, which will mark its forty-fifth anniversary in the year 2000, draws ever more guests from the far reaches of the world, while Walt's way has made such an impression on guests at Disney World that over 64 percent of them are repeat visitors!

Disney's financial record is equally impressive. It continually proves to be a solid investment. One thousand dollars invested in Disney stock in 1984, for example, would be worth $28,312 today, for a 29 percent compound annual growth rate. By comparison, a similar investment in Standard & Poor's Index of 500 stocks would be worth $8714, an 18 percent compound annual growth rate.

Such is the power of Walt's way: Dream. Believe. Dare. Do. You too can incorporate those words into your business vocabulary by following the ten beliefs that are at the heart of the Disney methodology:

- Give every member of your organization a chance to dream, and tap into the creativity those dreams embody.
- Stand firm on your beliefs and principles.
- Treat your customers like guests.
- Support, empower, and reward employees.
- Build long-term relationships with key suppliers and partners.
- Dare to take calculated risks in order to bring innovative ideas to fruition.
- Train extensively and constantly reinforce the company's culture.
- Align long-term vision with short-term execution.
- Use the storyboarding technique to solve planning and communication problems.
- Pay close attention to detail.

In each of the chapters that follow, you will see how one of these principles is being put into action daily by our clients, based on the Disney model. We will follow the Whirlpool Global No-Frost team in a series of sidebars as they experience and test the limits of each of the highlighted guidelines. These illustrations in practice, combined with a list of questions to ask and actions to take, will help you to make Walt's way your way.

We, however, are not suggesting that managers merely imitate Disney. Obviously, each company's and each individual's situation is different, and the wholesale adoption of another's methods is neither wise nor practical. But more importantly, Disney itself has won continued success by constantly reinventing its products to maintain superb quality. To imitate another and adopt a particular method lock, stock, and barrel implies a contentment with the status quo that flies in the face of everything Walt stood for.

Rather, we believe that gaining an understanding of the hows and whys of the Disney Company's growth and excellence and embracing the spirit of his four-pillared philosophy will enable businesspeople everywhere to innovate, make changes, and find their own unique pathways to continued success.

A Groundbreaking Project

In 1993, we became consultants to the Whirlpool Company during a restructuring that the Evansville Technology Center was preparing to undertake. In the process, one of our challenges was to set up teams for a variety of different projects. Among these, there was one team whose mission it was to design a radically new refrigerator for the company's global markets, which stretch from Latin America to Europe and Asia.

This story begins when the company decided that the refrigerator it sold abroad had to have a different design and be smaller than the refrigerator sold in the United States. In other words, this was, technologically, a completely new product, which needed to be built from a different set of blueprints.

The project was a groundbreaker from the beginning. Not only was the refrigerator a departure from previous products, but the approach to the implementation of its engineering, its design, and its marketing was a departure from accepted procedures. And the team we helped to establish to carry through these plans, from the first step to the last, was as much of a groundbreaker as the product itself.

We developed a close relationship with Jerry McColgin, who had been appointed leader of the team. An engineer by training who also had marketing experience, Jerry had led a team before. It had been a disappointing experience, but he had come away from it with a vision of how this global team should be created and how it would function. Later, when we reviewed the progress and the final success of the team, we concluded that here was a group of people, diverse in profession and in nationality, who exemplified everything that Walt Disney meant when he talked about his dreams, his beliefs, and his willingness to take risks in the execution of his vision. It is for this reason that we have decided to tell the story of this team, from its inception to its final celebration of success.

MAKE EVERYONE'S DREAMS COME TRUE

A dream is a wish your heart makes.

JIMINY CRICKET

It is no easy matter to convey a dream. Dreams are, by nature, deeply personal experiences. But true to his imaginative genius, Walt Disney was able to transform his dreams into stories that effectively articulated his vision to others. More importantly, the stories served to draw others into his fantasies, thereby marshaling the power of their collective creativity for the benefit of his dream.

In the early days, when the Disney Company was small, Walt used to call his five or six animators into his office to discuss an idea for a new film project. With dramatic effect, he would embark on a story—not a literal narrative account of his idea, but an ancient myth, perhaps, or some other related tale that conveyed the feelings and emotions behind his dream and his hope for the project's success. In short order, the master would capture the imaginations of his "cast members" ("employees" in the usual corporate parlance) and in the process stimulate the kind of excitement and commitment of minds and hearts that he well knew was necessary to turn Disney-size dreams into reality. For example, he insisted that the castle at Disneyland be built first—before anything else—so that this visual structure could help shape the vision and rally everyone around the dream he was trying to create (Fig. 2-1).

FIGURE 2-1.   The castle that helped shape the vision of Walt Disney's Dream.

He was such a vivid and persuasive storyteller that his listeners usually found themselves swept up—like Ward Kimball on the *Pinocchio* project—in a passionate endorsement of Walt's vision. Long before concrete plans were in place for the next movie or cartoon, before any budgets were prepared or administrative and engineering problems ironed out, Walt had established a team atmosphere around the forthcoming venture. Thus, he began nearly every new project with eager and enthusiastic participants, an enormous advantage in a process that often involved long hours of work, seven days a week.

Storytelling can be a powerful tool for focusing an organization on a particular problem or project and for unleashing employees' creativity by giving them the power to Dream. We have helped clients in a variety of industries tailor the technique to fit their particular situations. As you come to understand how this age-old art and other methods are used today by the Disney Company, and by many of our clients, you will begin to see how dreams can drive desired change.

DREAM RETREATS INSPIRE CREATIVITY

The use of storytelling to rally all project members around a vision is still an important element of the Disney approach, thanks to Walt's formation in the early 1950s of a creative group called "Imagineering." Organized during the building of Disneyland, the group's purpose is to carry on the Disney tradition by dreaming up new creative venues, such as the theme park attractions.

Today, there are approximately 2000 Imagineers at the five Disney theme parks. They are the inspiration for a concept that we call "Dream Retreats." As we tell our clients when we explain the Dream Retreat methodology, "If you can Dream it, you can Do it." Having employed this technique for many years, we know from experience that even seemingly frivolous, blue-sky notions can lead to realistic, yet innovative, outcomes.

When the Disney Company set out to build an additional water park at Disney World, for example, a small team met in the office of the team leader, a senior vice president, to get the project under way. The office was decorated with all manner of personal memorabilia, including those little glass snow domes that, when shaken, produce a flurry of swirling snowflakes.

Picking up a dome and shaking it, the vice president commented, "Too bad we can't make a park out of one of these." After a general pause, a team member asked, "Why not?" From that simple question, the team took off on the apparently impossible notion of building a ski resort in the sunshine of central Florida.

One artist sketched a picture of an alligator wearing earmuffs and careening down a slope on skis. Another drew a fanciful rendition of a winter resort enclosed in a snow dome. Not suitable for Florida, everyone agreed, but loath to discard the idea, they turned instead to the well-established Disney storytelling method and devised a tale based on a blizzard.

Here's how it developed: A capricious winter storm brought a heavy load of snow to Florida. An entrepreneur came along and built a ski resort. He did well until the weather returned to normal, melting the snow and turning the ski runs into rushing waterfalls. But the waterfalls were then turned into...what else?—water rides for adventurous athletes.

Using this fantasy story as their inspiration, Disney engineers and architects built the new water park and gave it the name Blizzard Beach.

Another example of this tried-and-true approach is when the Imagineers actually constructed a story to enhance the romance of Pleasure Island. To set the stage for the envisioned experience, they wove an entirely fictitious tale about the history of the location, to wit: The land originally belonged to a seafaring adventurer, Merryweather Pleasure, who settled there to build a successful canvas and sail-making company. Pleasure built a thriving industrial complex. As the years passed and Merryweather Pleasure listened to the stories told by visiting seagoing types and other adventurers, his nostalgia for his past proved too strong to resist. He sailed away from Pleasure Island forever, leaving his company in the hands of two sons. They were lazy and indifferent to their father's legacy, however, and gradually the warehouses fell into disrepair.

Imagineers refurbished the island, turning its rundown warehouses into exciting restaurants and nightclubs designed to reflect the regional themes of Pleasure's functional buildings. Once again, the district bustles with activity of world travelers who come together in the spirit of fun and adventure, a tradition established here a century ago.

But the real importance of both the Pleasure Island and the Blizzard Beach examples is that they united team members around whimsical notions that piqued their creative playfulness and drew them completely into the visions for the projects. Repeating and embellishing the fantastical stories engaged team members in a way that discussion of budgets and staffing problems could never have done. A team linked by a central idea, even one built on whimsy, is better able to tackle the mundane matters that must be dealt with in order to bring a project to completion. It's the primary reason that Walt Disney wanted the castle at Disneyland to be the first building constructed.

The Cincinnati-based restaurant Hotel Discovery developed an inspiring legend as well. The legend of Hotel Discovery is this: "Once upon a time, seven years before the turn of the new century 2000 A.D., a private idea created an imaginary place where things of adventure, distant travel, and time had no limitations. The place would be a mind's-eye observatory from which one could embark on an odyssey to the four realms of wonder—adventure, imagination, invention, and exploration. The idea envisioned tastes of great food and drinks from near and afar, a place that offered overwhelming hospitality while being surrounded by the mysterious things of myth and legend. It was to be a place where the likes of Leonardo da Vinci, Jules Verne, Thomas Edison, Frank Lloyd Wright, Walt Disney, and other freelance mythmakers would have hung out, a place where reality was always an intruder. Welcome to Hotel Discovery."

At first blush, it might seem, particularly to the most literal-minded, that this kind of storytelling approach has merit only for those companies involved in the entertainment business. Not so. In our work with clients, we have observed the many ways in which practical lessons can be derived from stories woven out of subject matter closely related to an organization's specific business interests.

In one instance, we worked with a client who was attempting to transform his company's culture by discarding old ways and embracing a new set of values. As part of the change process, a group of employees was asked to write an imaginary newspaper story reporting the company's triumphant turnaround. The chroniclers were told to describe the winning ways embraced by the company and how they were implemented.

The purpose of this exercise was to force the group to think about how forthcoming cultural changes should be developed, how they would affect the company, and how these employees personally would execute them. A number of different scenarios emerged; some were nuts-and-bolts pieces, others had a streak of fantasy about them, but all evidenced an understanding of the company's goals.

DREAM RETREATS FOSTER PARTICIPATION

Walt Disney instinctively knew that participation by cast members in the development of a new "show" gave them a sense of commitment, both to the project in question and to the company itself. Judging from the extremely low turnover rates at his namesake company, we can say that Walt's instincts were, as always, right on target. Whereas a 100 percent turnover rate is the norm at most theme parks, rank-and-file turnover at Disney is less than 30 percent. And within the company's management ranks, turnover is less than 6 percent.

What's more, everything we have learned in working with companies worldwide lends support to the validity of Walt's inclusive approach. Employees everywhere, whether in China or India or Italy, basically agree on what is important and what is offensive in a corporate culture. They dislike arrogance on the part of management, and they desperately want real, two-way communication that includes them in planning and product development.

Never is employee participation more important than when a company decides to embark on a program of change. Perhaps customer service is suffering or employee turnover is reaching unacceptable levels or the product offering is tired and stale. Whatever it is that provides the eventual impetus, one thing will be clear: The old way is no longer working, and a new framework of operation is needed. When that happens, companies invite disaster if they don't involve frontline employees in the process. As we have seen so many times in working with our clients, such involvement is a key part of communicating with people during times of change.

A Dream Retreat has proved to be an ideal way of helping companies initiate needed change. Besides involving employees in strategy and facilitating their understanding of the vision and direction the company is pursuing, a Dream Retreat environment propels participants into a world of new ideas that often spark innovative solutions to the problems at hand.

The retreats, which can last anywhere from three days to a week, are conducted away from the company premises. We have found that off-site gatherings are a great way to break down barriers and begin the planning process for the kind of change that ultimately revolutionizes a culture. When people are removed from daily routines and placed in an atmosphere that encourages free expression of their dreams, amazing ideas begin to emerge and flourish. Dreaming in this context is not a solitary occupation; participants bat around project ideas, argue, laugh, and brainstorm solutions as a group.

Storytelling is always encouraged at the Dream Retreats, but occasionally a new client will balk at learning and practicing the technique. Such reluctance is understandable. After all, we are proposing a radical departure from the customary business procedure. In the traditional environment, employees are informed of a new project when most of the preliminary details are in place. They are told who will work on a project, what the budget is, and what the deadlines are. To suggest that management invite employees into the strategy and planning process through storytelling is at odds with received wisdom.

Most of our clients, however, are open-minded and willing to experiment, once they understand that communicating their vision is pivotal to innovation and project success. We tell them that if they want employees to get behind a corporate vision, they have to let those employees know what that vision is. We often think of a former client that literally kept its strategic plan under lock and key. Employees cannot possibly help advance specific goals if they aren't privy to the overall plan.

New clients sometimes have difficulty in understanding the basic value of Dream Retreats. "What will my company gain from such an idea?" we are asked. "It sounds like some kind of a vacation to me. Everyone will probably just want to play golf."

But a Dream Retreat is only a vacation from operating in the old, less-than-optimal style. In reality, a Dream Retreat involves a lot of hard work and grappling with tough decisions. Employees are removed from the administrative details that hamper their creativity at the office so that they can focus on strategy and planning in a fresh, innovative way.

THE DREAM RETREAT IN ACTION

While disabusing our clients of the notion that a Dream Retreat is a break from work, we want them to understand the excitement that such an experience generates. The power of the collective intelligence and the power of teaming amid a spirit of fun creates a unique atmosphere that is rich with inventive possibilities.

One of our favorite examples is Whirlpool's Global No-Frost team (featured in the sidebars at the end of each chapter). In 1994, this team was formed to create a new international product that would require building a plant in India. The team consisted of members from India, China, Brazil, Italy, Canada, and the United States. Under the old way of doing business, leaders from the six areas involved would have gotten together to devise a plan, then taken pieces of that plan back to their respective countries and started working separately.

This time, though, things were to be different. Instead of following marching orders issued from the top, an empowered team was charged with examining the options and coming up with an agenda. Team leader Jerry McColgin wasted no time in setting the tone for how he wanted his group to tackle the work ahead. His first order of business was to insist on a new layout for the team's office space at its Indiana facility. Out went the walls, the cubicles, the compartmentalized look to create a space that resembled an old-fashioned newsroom: open, convivial, and barrier-free.

The project officially got under way with a five-day Dream Retreat for 40 people from all over the world. There, in the dead of an Indiana winter, the Global No-Frost team assembled its collective talent.

The retreat began with people talking about their personal dreams and their sense of the team's mission. The individual interests of each sector were weighed against the overall goals of the company as the team strove to achieve a realistic balance for the project. As the five days unfolded, however, something exciting and gratifying began to happen: The barriers between the various functional areas started to crumble. Technicians accepted responsibility for engineering tasks; engineers listened attentively to marketing concerns; marketers assumed the critical business role of evaluating suppliers. Even the usually standoffish finance people willingly jumped into the trenches with purchasing and marketing folks. The flow of ideas became a flood. By the end of the retreat, everyone was working together for the common good of the team.

The Dream Retreat was an essential first step on a project that ended up surpassing everyone's initial expectations. Never before have new Whirlpool products arrived on the market so quickly. That's because the Global No-Frost team met every deadline and achieved every goal. When in the middle of the project team members found that they needed to lower costs further than originally planned in order to increase competitive position, they rallied to the cause and did it without cutting quality. And here's the icing on the cake: The entire project came in *under* budget.

It's not unusual for our clients to credit a Dream Retreat for keeping costs in check.

As Brian Hartke, manager of project engineering at the Bristol-Myers Squibb Company's Mead Johnson Nutritional division, aptly points out: "If you change something in the planning stage, it costs you a dollar. If you change something in the design phase, it costs you ten dollars. If you change something after the plant is built, it costs you a hundred dollars." A Dream Retreat increases the opportunities for figuring out what's needed early in the process, before you spend a lot of change for the change.

In 1993, before Mead Johnson Nutritional division began constructing the world's largest production facility for infant-formula powder in Zeeland, Michigan, Hartke brought his diverse construction team together for a Dream Retreat at a hotel in Holland, Michigan. The team members, both workers and suppliers, "really got to know one another there," Hartke says. "They put together plans through formal and informal conversations." And because of that initial interaction, the team continued face-to-face meetings throughout the project. End result: The plant was completed on time and on budget.

Another example of the value of a Dream Retreat occurred when we worked with British Petroleum Ltd. in 1990. But far more than just a single project was at stake in this instance. As the worldwide oil company bluntly admitted, "Nothing short of a complete overhaul...was needed." The company was too autocratic. It was strangling in red tape. Turf consciousness was impeding efficiency, and the company was hierarchical to the point of paralysis. Not surprisingly, employee morale was also frighteningly low.

"The business climate is challenging," a company report concluded, "and only the best oil companies will survive into the 21st century." At the rate the octogenarian BP was going (the company was founded in 1909), that it would live to see the next millennium was far from certain. Old oil fields were declining, and because of fiercely competitive conditions, new ones were tougher to find. Costs were escalating. And skilled technicians were becoming scarcer.

To remedy the situation, the company had an ambitious organizationwide innovation initiative. In fact, it envisioned an entirely new corporate culture, one where a more partici-patory environment would give employees the freedom and responsibility, within certain limits, to make decisions. A far cry from the rigid command-and-control policies of the past, such an initiative would be quite a change if the company could pull it off.

Bill launched a Dream Retreat that produced a major turnaround in day-to-day office procedures. Managers became visible and present for their employees, not deskbound behind closed doors. No longer were meetings run from on high, with orders handed down and questions distinctly unwelcome. Teams replaced the previous hierarchy throughout the company. Training and coaching of employees was the order of the day. To bring the message of this new company vision to all employees, BP held town-hall meetings.

Something of what this change-management initiative has meant to British Petroleum can be discerned from one small incident. Prior to the overhaul, a team of high-powered geologists and engineers at the company's U.S. exploration headquarters in Anchorage, Alaska, produced a monthly report for the president that analyzed seismic data and estimated potential oil reserves at the Prudhoe Bay field. It was a complex, time-consuming task that took energy away from other vital duties.

As part of the new atmosphere of empowerment, the scientists and engineers scrutinized the process, evaluated its costs, and discovered that an inordinate number of worker-hours were being devoted to it. Then they asked why. Was the monthly process really vital to the interests of the company? Or was it being done just in case the president happened to ask for an estimate of the latest oil reserves? They made their case to the president, who agreed that since the report was, at best, an estimate, an assessment every three months was entirely sufficient. The savings in time and money were considerable.

Although the revitalized BP is still evolving, old habits have been eliminated, and the refrain "we have always done it this way" is rarely, if ever, heard these days. In June of 1998, *Industry Week* reported that British Petroleum expects 20 percent more oil from its oil-production operations in Alaska. Officials reported that reduced costs and technological advances have made expansion on the North Slope feasible. Moreover, as the Prudhoe Bay example illustrates, management is upholding its end of the bargain by supporting empowered employees who make smart, solid recommendations. And as for the bottom line, John Browne, BP's group chief executive, speaking to the financial community recently, recounted sustained improvement in cost reduction and volume increases in the five years from 1992 through 1996. During that period, Browne said, profits grew by more than $3 billion.

TRACKING GOOD IDEAS

Dream Retreats offer the fastest and most productive way to achieve flexibility and openness within a company's ranks. But once people become accustomed to acknowledging their own creative powers, you must implement a system outside the retreat setting that encourages them to bring their ideas to management.

When Walt Disney was at the helm of the company, everyone was invited to voice their opinions and to make suggestions—in fact, not just invited but *required.* The corporate hierarchy dissolved when it came to offering ideas for improving a movie script, a theme park ride, or an animated sequence. Anyone could bring suggestions for cartoons and features to Walt himself. Basically, the same holds true today, but the size of the company makes a casual approach impractical. The company does provide regular opportunities to harvest good ideas from all corners of the organization, however.

In a thrice-yearly event known as the Gong Show, named after a television program popular in the 1970s and '80s, animators, secretaries, and anyone else who thinks he or she has a good idea can formally make a pitch to a panel of top brass that includes CEO Michael Eisner, vice chairman of the board Roy Disney, executive vice president of animation Tom Schumacher, and president of the animation division Peter Schneider.

On average, 40 ideas are presented as succinctly as possible. It is a tough milieu because the listeners at the table provide immediate and honest reactions. "You must have immediate communication and not worry about people's egos and feelings," Schneider says. "If you do that enough and people do not get fired or demoted, they begin to understand that no matter how good, bad, or indifferent the idea, it can be expressed, accepted, and considered."[2]

The Gong Show is a valuable learning experience for many employees, helping them to see why one idea works and another doesn't. It is also an experience that enhances the atmosphere of freedom—freedom both to dream and to share those dreams with the company's highest authorities. And by creating an environment in which people feel safe to express their creativity, the Disney Company is giving itself the immeasurable benefit of literally thousands of good ideas— ideas so good that they have sewn the seeds for most of Disney's animated features. *Hercules,* for example, grew from an animator's idea that a man is judged by his inner strength and not his outer strength. Though the story line ended up changing, the basic premise stood and the movie went on to be a commercial success.

Not long ago, we were showing an executive from British Petroleum around Disney World. "What a pity that Walt Disney did not live to see this place," he remarked.

"But he did see it," we said. "That's why it's here."

Obviously, the Disney Company is involved in an industry that is equal parts art and commerce. But there is no industry, no matter how basic, that couldn't benefit from injecting a dollop of Walt's unfettered visionary spirit into too-often sclerotic corporate veins. Many of the greatest figures in American business—from Thomas Edison to Bill Gates—have been dreamers, and it's no accident that Steven Spielberg, an American icon approaching Disney status, has named his new company DreamWorks SKG. Companies *must* give themselves permission to dream. Whether or not they come with an equivalent of Disney World in which to showcase their fantasies, the simple act of letting imaginations run free will increase creativity and innovation.

Any kind of cultural change comes slowly, and the powerful transformation to be fueled by adoption of the Dream concept is no exception. If your company is large and if old attitudes and methods are firmly entrenched, it may take three to five years for the new culture to take permanent root. However, we have worked with organizations that began realizing improvements in service and productivity within a few months.

In spite of visible short-term gains, however, some companies will still voice concern over the slowness of the overall transformation process, at which point we relate the story of the hundredth monkey.

In the 1950s, on the Japanese island of Koshima, scientists studying macaque monkeys dropped sweet potatoes in the sand. The monkeys liked the taste of the potatoes, but they found the sand to be unpleasant. One innovative monkey discovered that washing the potatoes in seawater eliminated the grit and made the potatoes taste better. She quickly taught this to her mother and several of her playmates.

As one would expect, other young monkeys in the troop were soon imitating this monkey's intelligent behavior. Then after several years had passed, the last lines of resistance were finally eroded after one particular incident. Legend states that one morning, a certain number of monkeys were washing their potatoes. The exact number is not known, but for the sake of the story, we'll say that it was 99. Later that morning, one more monkey learned to wash his potato. As the day progressed, each of the remaining dirty-potato-eating monkeys began washing his potato until, by evening, every monkey in the troop had developed a taste for clean potatoes!

A similar transference of learned behavior also occurs in organizations that are undergoing change. Although the exact number may vary, a point is reached where, if only one more person adopts a new set of values, the synergy is so great that nearly everyone else will internalize the behavior too.

Whether or not this story is legend or fact, there are several lessons that we can learn from the hundredth monkey story.

- First, total transformation takes time. In the case of the Koshima monkeys, it took several years.
- Second, the benefits of transformation must be real. Just as the monkeys enjoyed the benefits of eating clean potatoes, employees must be able to experience real gains as they adopt cultural change.

- Third, management must consistently model the desired behavior. The innovative monkeys continued to exhibit the potato-washing method before other members of the troop. Be persistent.

- Fourth, there must be top management commitment at the outset. When the first monkey learned to wash her food, she taught the skill to her mother and to a handful of adults. The adult converts provided positive feedback by embracing and using the newly learned skill. Without their early commitment, it's unlikely that the entire troop transformation would ever have taken place.

Time, persistence, and commitment are the keys to long-term benefits. And remember, as we always say, "The first 99 are the hardest!"

* * *

The Dream concept is first and foremost a visionary undertaking, but both management and employees must keep the overall organizational values firmly in mind as they plan new strategies and set about implementing cultural change. In other words, if innovation is to be successful over the long term, it's imperative that a company remains true to itself. In the chapter that follows, we explore what Walt Disney did to ensure that his dreams and those of his company remained firmly grounded in a set of basic core beliefs. And we examine how a Disneylike adherence to a values-based approach is helping other companies to achieve bottom-line success.

Questions to Ask
- Does top management acknowledge that the process of "dreaming" inspires creativity?
- Does top management understand that adopting new paradigms takes time and commitment; are they willing to see the transformation through to its fruition?

- Do your teams participate in off-site retreats where they engage in strategy and planning?
- Do you utilize the storytelling technique in planning projects?

Actions to Take
- Hold annual, off-site Dream Retreats for top management and all departmental teams.
- Unleash creativity by encouraging all employees to participate in structured dreaming to solve problems and develop solutions.
- Engage employees in developing the story of what the organization could be like in five years. From these stories, develop a vision of what the company will look like five years from now.
- Determine the values the organization must embrace to achieve its vision.
- Communicate the organizational vision and values to your coworkers, customers, suppliers, managers, directors, and stockholders.
- Display the organizational vision and values in prominent places throughout the company.
- Use the storytelling technique as a method to assist teams in launching projects.

THE MANY GOALS OF THE GLOBAL NO-FROST TEAM

When Jerry McColgin agreed to take on the job as leader of the team, he drew on past experience. He had headed up a team whose structure and way of operating were entirely company-mandated. "We did not have full-time dedicated resources," Jerry explained, "the engineers on whom I was dependent actually reported to the engineering department in their respective locations."* Furthermore, he had been asked to work with a lot of part-time people. The peo-

*Jerry McColgin. Phone interview with Wordworks, April 1998.

ple on the project had lacked cohesion and a unity of purpose. If Jerry came to them and explained what should be done, they would agree, but when they discussed it with their department heads, the answer was, "That's all very good and fine, but here's how we're really going to do it." It had been an international project with no contribution from the targeted markets. As a result, the project failed.

McColgin was determined that there would not be another failure. When the company tried to tell him how the project was to be run, he dug in his heels. He believed that he now knew how to create a successful team. This time, he brought together an international group of people and announced that there would be no part-time participation and no divided loyalties. From the outset, the team would be unified in a shared vision.

The company was also building a new plant in Pune, India, to manufacture the product. Among its many goals, the team was to design the equipment, figure out costs, and plan the marketing, all for a number of different countries. All these countries needed representation on the team, whose numbers included engineers, designers, and finance experts speaking different languages and coming from dissimilar cultures. Style differences between the members were apparent at the beginning of the project. Yet people from Brazil, China, Italy, and India would all be sitting next to each other every day and working together. Their main goal was to develop the model for a common refrigerator that could be built around the world. As a selling point, it was also to be manufactured with a frost-free freezing compartment—hence the name of the team, the Global No-Frost Team.

YOU BETTER BELIEVE IT

When you believe a thing, believe it implicitly and unquestionably.[3]

WALT DISNEY

When Walt Disney was still an infant, his family moved from Chicago to a farm in Marceline, Missouri, about 100 miles east of Kansas City. Farm life is hard and demanding, and a growing boy, then as now, always has chores to do. But after the barn was mucked out or the apples picked, young Walt would lie in the grass and gaze up at the Missouri sky or watch insects and butterflies flit overhead. These were memories that he treasured all his life.

From those early years growing up in a rural environment, Disney formed beliefs and values that stuck with him throughout his life and from which he never deviated. His love of nature, handsomely depicted in numerous animated and live action films, surely can be traced to those experiences, as can the basic foursquare family values that still guide the Walt Disney Company today.

Perfectly complementing Walt's firmly held beliefs was the philosophy expressed by his brother, Roy: "When values are clear, decisions are easy."[4] Together, these precepts formed what is, in effect, the Disney company's mantra: "Live your beliefs"—or what we simply call *Believe*.

Carrying that theme a step further, we might add that if "seeing is believing," then the unparalleled success of the Walt

Disney Company is convincing proof of the power inherent in the Believe concept. But as our clients know, before success can be achieved, a personal set of core values must be formalized, communicated to the company at large, and actually lived day to day. Disney has shown the way.

BUILT ON BELIEFS

Early on, Walt infused his work with the personal core values that also came to define his company. In his initial Mickey Mouse cartoons, for example, the character of Mickey was overly rambunctious and even a bit crude at times. But Walt quickly recognized that such behavior would never do if Mickey was to be embraced by audiences young and old. The mouse would have to reflect the solid values held by his viewers. Thus, Walt saw to it that honesty, reliability, loyalty, and respect for people as individuals—the same principles he would espouse within the company—formed the essence of Mickey's character.

In more recent times, the Gong Show idea that grew into the 1997 movie *Hercules* was approved precisely because it fit so perfectly with the Disney Company's core values. Inspired by the tale of the mythical Greek hero, the film idea was based on the premise that a person should be judged not only on his or her outer strength but by inner moral strength as well.

"The core value puts process into creativity," says Peter Schneider, president of the animation division. That's the way the Disney Company sees it. Thus, the first step in any project, moviemaking or otherwise, is to determine what core value is being promoted. When it came to the making of *The Hunchback of Notre Dame*, for example, the creative team decided, after much discussion and soul-searching, that the core value of the story was self-value. They had to agree on this premise before they could go forward.

We are convinced that a refusal to compromise values is necessary if an organization is to scale the heights. What's important is not necessarily the content of a company's core ideology, but rather how consistently that ideology is expressed and lived.

The Levi Strauss Company, for example, has shown an extraordinary commitment to core values in its everyday operations. The original maker of the quintessentially American blue jeans has long enjoyed a reputation as a good place to work, and it is known for its commitment to empowering workers and compensating them generously. In addition, it has formalized its beliefs in its mission and aspiration statements, and in 1991 became the first multinational company to set down guidelines governing business partners abroad. Its aim is to assure that workplace standards and business practices in foreign operations are in line with company policies.

When tough competition in the mid-1990s forced the company to close 11 of its 37 factories and lay off more than 6000 employees, its first major cutback in more than 140 years of operation, the experience was an understandably painful one for management. In characteristic fashion, the company set about making careful preparations to ease the trauma of the layoffs. Each affected employee was given eight months' notice, and $31,000 per laid-off employee was put aside to help facilitate job searches. The company worked with unions and with local governments to get retraining programs off the ground quickly. Every step taken by Levi Strauss was an expression of its core values and its basic respect for each individual in its workforce.

"Our people will know," Robert Haas, the CEO, said, "that if bad things happen, they will be treated much better than they would be elsewhere."[5] In the midst of extremely difficult times, both financially and culturally, the company held firm to its values while also making sure that its product continued to be the best it could be.

Offering your customers the best product or service means not only establishing certain values as Walt Disney did but also having the good sense to recognize when the situation dictates that one value takes precedence over another. Walt insisted on safety, courtesy, the good show, and efficiency, but he also expected common sense to prevail. First and foremost, it was never permissible to jeopardize a guest's safety in any way, at any time, no matter what the attraction or performance. That meant that if a child was in danger of falling out of a Jungle Boat, for example, courtesy, show, and efficiency temporarily fell by the wayside until the situation was corrected. Or if someone was having difficulty understanding directions, courtesy to that guest won out over show and efficiency.

By the same token, the concept of the good show carried more weight than did a desire for efficient operations. Excellence at every level was, and is, the watchword at Disney, because Walt believed that only by giving audiences the best of entertainment could he live up to his core values of honesty and reliability. He refused to take short cuts merely to inflate the bottom line.

Just as Walt refused to accept a substandard *Pinocchio* even though reworking the characters significantly bumped up the cost, so, too, are certain extravagances countenanced on a regular basis today because they greatly enhance the show. The exquisite topiaries in the theme parks are one example. Because it takes three to ten years to grow and shape the trees to look like Dumbo, Mickey, and other characters, it would obviously be more efficient and less costly to install plastic statues instead. But the topiaries add natural beauty that imparts a greater level of excellence to the entire show; plus, they are enjoyed and photographed by thousands of guests.

In the end, of course, Disney's adherence to basic beliefs and the company's willingness to spend time and money to deliver the excellence it values have been amply rewarded by the huge success of its films, theme parks, and other ventures.

FORMALIZING THE BELIEFS

To ensure that employees at all levels would be guided by his beliefs and his visionary sense of purpose, Walt Disney fostered what amounted to an almost cultlike atmosphere. His passionate belief in the need to instill a company culture led him to set up a formal training program that has come to be known as the Disney University.

The program, which stresses the uniqueness of the company and the importance of adhering to its values, came into being as a result of a situation Walt encountered when Disneyland opened in 1955. Initially, he hired an outside security firm and leased out the parking concession. "I soon realized my mistake," he said, explaining that with "outside help" he couldn't effectively convey his idea of hospitality.[6] That's when the company began recruiting and training every one of its employees.

Walt wanted each and every cast member to embrace the basic Disney belief of courtesy to customers, of treating them like guests in their own homes. "I tell the security officers," he once said, "that they are never to consider themselves cops. They are here to help people."[7] Setting up a security force and training the officers in the company's values and beliefs was no doubt more expensive than outsourcing the job, but monetary considerations took a backseat to ensuring that everyone exhibited courtesy.

Every new cast member must spend several days in "Traditions" training before starting the job. During this orientation period, the Disney culture is communicated through powerful storytelling. The value of the program was proven several years ago when cost-cutting corporate types decided to reduce the training period by just one day. Complaints from supervisors throughout the parks began to pour in. "The quality of guest service is not the quality we had last season," they said. "Have you changed the hiring policy?"[8]

Top management took a close look at the process and found out that only one thing had changed. The missing day of Traditions training was added back in and the complaints stopped. Instilling the culture takes time, but anyone who has visited a Disney theme park is well aware of what the training program brings to the show: Questions are answered courteously, crowd control is unobtrusive, and cast members at every turn willingly go the extra mile to make each guest's dreams come true.

On the face of it, our advice to strictly adhere to a formalized set of beliefs and values may sound naïve and unsophisticated, if not downright impractical. It may come across as the kind of do-good counsel you read about in an inspirational pamphlet. But this is not theoretical; it is practical and proven in the stories of companies that have adopted the Believe concept.

One company we have worked with which displays a strict adherence to its own values is Lensing Wholesale. A long-standing, family-owned business in Evansville, Indiana, which distributes building products, Lensing's strong family values are transparent to all who enter its doors. While the company provides outstanding service to all its customers, we were especially impressed to witness the determination of Lensing's President, Joe Theby, to formalize the company's values and mission in written statements at our recommendation. Many family businesses ignore this important step, believing that employees are already clear about company values, since they have been in place since the company's formation.

In formalizing Lensing values, Joe's first priority was to define the word "value." At Lensing, a value is "a desirable standard of personal conduct or action; a worthy trait." Joe and his team decided on 11 core values, ranging from quality to customer relations.

At one company meeting which we attended, Joe gave a heartfelt speech to his employees about the value of customers and great service. During the meeting, he said that anybody could put up a warehouse and stock it with wholesale building products, but few could gain a reputation as truly understanding their customers and being there when the customers needed them. Illustrating the importance Lensing places on its ability to do just this, the company's customer relations value incorporates the following aspects: to deal well with customers; display honesty, integrity, and a sincere concern for their needs; remember names and faces; and maintain poise, integrity, and confidence during all interactions. A firm belief in this value and a strict adherence to its concept is what comes through loud and clear when speaking to any Lensing employee.

THE LONG-TERM MENTALITY

Again and again, we have witnessed how companies are strengthened when they impart a clear understanding of their basic beliefs and core values. For one thing, a set of bedrock values gives a sense of security to all stakeholders and serves as a touchstone for company leaders. Although Walt Disney often teetered on the edge of bankruptcy, he was able to stay focused on his goals for the future because he believed so strongly in what he was trying to do and how he was trying to do it.

We call that the long-term mentality, but unfortunately, many companies manifest just the opposite. Their satisfaction with present achievements evidences a short-term view of the world and causes them to rest on their laurels—often with disastrous results. The Xerox Corporation, for example, squandered its lead in the copying-machine market to the Japanese and found itself left with only a 7 percent market share before it began a turnaround in the 1980s. So, too, the Raytheon Company, which invented the microwave oven in 1947; Raytheon now has an insignificant share of the microwave market. The point is that even companies with innovative product ideas can be paralyzed by a short-term mentality that causes them to end up on the losing side.

It is a measure of Walt Disney's certain belief in his product that he was also able early on to envision a continuing demand for his cartoons and movies. With brilliant foresight, Disney decided on a rerelease policy that would bring his movies to a new generation of viewers at five- and ten-year intervals. But again, Walt's prescience was dependent on his adherence to core values. He intended his movies to last—and last they did, because he insisted on excellence.

Disney's cartoons and animated films look as fresh today as when Walt's animators created them. That's because he paid attention to even the smallest detail of production and combined the most skillful drawings with the best available technology. At a time when many animators were using six to eight drawings per second, for instance, Disney insisted on 24 drawings. (All animation went to 24 frames per second with the advent of sound, but the superiority of the Disney technique can be better understood by comparing it to today's average Saturday morning cartoon. Even though these cartoons run 24 frames per second, they use only six to eight *drawings* per second, which means the same drawing is repeated three to four times. Disney animation provides 24 unique drawings per second.)

Equally important to Walt's long-term planning was the fact that he never lost sight of his market and the family values that endure. Rereleased Disney films have made as much, if not more, money on their second release than they did on the first.

Today, the company applies the same policy to the video market. When a Disney movie is released on video, it stays on the store shelf for six months and is then withdrawn for a specified period. People who don't buy it during the Disney-designated time frame simply have to wait until the next time it's back on the shelf. Tightly controlling distribution allows Disney to market its product over and over to succeeding generations of viewers. Since 1992, according to *Video Store Magazine,* six of the eight top-selling videos were Disney videos, with *Snow White and the Seven Dwarfs* and *The Lion King* tied for number 1.

The long-term mentality is apparent throughout the Disney empire—in its real estate transactions, for example. Although Walt was never interested in real estate as a personal investment, he took a wholly different approach when it came to his theme parks. And his experience with Disneyland only served to harden an already instinctual tendency to take the long view.

In 1954, when Walt bought the 160-acre Anaheim, California, parcel for Disneyland, he was constrained from acquiring additional land by limited financial resources, the already heavy debt he was incurring, and estimates of what it would cost to build his park. But Walt never ceased to regret not buying more land, especially as his extraordinarily successful park became hemmed in by tawdry fast-food outlets and motels. He vowed that he would not make the same mistake twice.

When it came time to plan for Disney World, Walt was not hampered by such monetary constraints. He bought 29,500 acres of Florida real estate for an average price of $200 an acre. Less than half of that acreage is being used today, while the remainder has risen in value to more than $1 million an acre. Selling off the undeveloped land would bring more than $10 billion into corporate coffers.

Why doesn't the company sell the Florida acreage? Because such a sale would be at odds with the Disney long-term mentality. Still adhering to Walt's beliefs, the company is looking ahead to expansion that will further upgrade the show. The theme-park business, after all, is driven by a need to constantly offer new attractions that will entice both first-time and repeat guests.

Michael Eisner made it clear that short-term gains are not what Disney is about when he said at an industry conference in 1997: "I'm not looking for some outrageous, ridiculous multiple that blows in the wind or gets battered by changes in the economy. I hope people like the company, but I don't want to promise them nirvana."

LEADERSHIP FOR THE LONG TERM

In today's business world, where technology is driving an accelerated pace of change, a long-term mentality is a must for survival. But not everyone recognizes this imperative, as evidenced by some of our consulting experiences. The one-man roadblock we encountered when we began working with a large *Fortune* 500 manufacturer is a case in point.

We had asked a top management team to formalize the plans and specifications for an initiative intended to take their division into the future. The team worked for three months on the plan, meeting one full day a week to establish their values, decide on the organizational structure, and determine how best to communicate the vision underlying the plan.

The plans were great, but the boss failed to act on them. Sure, he *talked* about what he was going to do, but he never, as the saying goes, *walked the talk*. No changes were made until the boss was transferred and a young engineer named Steve was installed in his place.

Suddenly, plans turned into actions. Working together with his planning team, Steve established four subteams charged with developing new technologies, providing back-up systems and facilities support to engineers, improving processes, and empowering teams and individuals. Another group set about redesigning the work space to facilitate better communication.

It is worth noting that none of these changes were part of any kind of overall directive from corporate headquarters. In fact, about the only thing in the way of change that emanated from headquarters was an annual gesture amounting to little more than calling in a consultant who prepared brochures and produced videos touting the value of some "new" culture.

Recently, headquarters had issued another new cultural initiative. This time it included a management kickoff meeting at which a "talking-head" video was shown to communicate the importance of getting everyone on board with the high-performance principles. Steve's division was apathetic about the whole thing—and understandably so.

"It's almost an insult," some said, "when we've already been practicing these principles for years." These team members knew that Steve embodied the vision, and under his leadership they had achieved what the rest of the company was still contemplating. They had been living the vision.

The key element in this situation was the presence of a well-respected leader with a clear, long-term mentality. He had, in effect, become a pioneer in the company. What a contrast between Steve and his predecessor, who not only lacked vision himself but couldn't even muster the energy to implement the ideas generated by his staff.

Our experience working with Abbey Press further confirmed that leaders who exhibit strongly held beliefs are the key to solid achievement. Abbey Press, which publishes inspirational books and sells religious merchandise, is run by Benedictine monks with the support of a secular staff.

At our initial meeting to discuss a new cultural initiative, the executives from the Press told us that they had heard about "total quality" and were eager to find out how it could be applied to their venture. Father Carl, the general manager, was particularly enthusiastic: "I knew we needed a different organization for the '90s and for the 21st century so that we could compete, keep our costs down," he says. His recognition that the success the organization had enjoyed for many years was beginning to wane prompted a fresh look at how to better satisfy customers.

However, our work with Father Carl and the Press was interrupted when we were involved in an airplane crash from which we barely escaped with our lives. We were both deeply moved when, during our hospital stay, we received a book from the Abbey Press staff and a note saying, "We are holding off our implementation until you return." Their belief in Father Carl's vision and their commitment to continue despite the delay imposed by our accident actually hastened our recovery.

Once back at work, we met with the board of directors of the Press and received approval to move forward. We organized a Dream Retreat for Father Carl and his staff. At the end of our three-day retreat, John Wilson, Father Carl's boss, who had been invited at Carl's request, jumped to his feet to declare somewhat sheepishly that he had been reluctant to attend the meeting. Three times in the days before the retreat, Wilson had been ready to pick up the phone and say that he and his staff would not be able to participate after all. Only his respect for Father Carl, who had voiced great excitement about the teamwork a new culture would bring, stopped Wilson from backing out.

Now Wilson was admitting how close he had come to making "a big mistake." After experiencing the Dream Retreat, he, too, was pleased and excited about the initiative and, in fact, wanted to bring the process to "the Hill," the term used to describe the various administrative functions that support the monastery.

One step had led to another in the unfolding of events. Father Carl's preretreat enthusiasm and his strong belief in the value of the change process had captured John Wilson's attention. After listening carefully and participating in the retreat, Wilson came to share Father Carl's enthusiasm. Through the leadership of these two, the plan for cultural change was communicated to the entire staff and to the board of directors and has now taken root throughout the organization.

BELIEVING IN INNOVATION

For Walt Disney, innovation was second nature, which is one of the reasons he was such a strong leader. Our definition of leadership, in fact, revolves around the ability to create and manage an environment for innovation. But as we've discovered over the years, too many managers find the idea of innovation downright scary; some even react as if we are suggesting a revolution without a cause. Another common reaction is that of the CEO or vice president who, while looking completely self-satisfied when we mention innovation, remarks, "We have one of the best R&D divisions of any company in the country. It's their job to come up with new products."

Our response to this statement is that R&D product innovations rarely change the whole culture of a company. Innovation is a three-legged animal that must encompass product, service, *and* process. In terms of product, innovation not only means making something entirely new but perhaps rethinking how the old works or how it is used. Process innovation leads to improvements in the way the product is produced, and service innovation changes the way the product is integrated into the entire organization.

As we remind our clients, the goal of every organization should be to encourage innovation at all levels and in all functional areas, not just R&D. But in order for everyone in the company to become an innovator, the leadership has to be committed to creating an atmosphere in which people and teams are motivated to achieve team goals while still maintaining respect for one another's personal values.

And what exactly does an innovative environment look like? For one thing, there is no such thing as "crazy." Radical departure from the old ways is often precisely what's needed if you are going to come up with solutions to customer problems. In 1937, Walt Disney sent Jake Day to the woods of Maine to take hundreds of photos and make numerous drawings in preparation for the production of *Bambi,* which would be released in 1942. "Crazy" is probably one of the kindest words that many of Walt's contemporaries in the animated film business used to describe such a radical and innovative approach to capturing the magic of the forest. But Disney let his beliefs guide his actions regardless of what the naysayers thought.

The message is: Go the extra mile yourself and encourage your people to do the same. Let them know that it's okay to take risks, to let their off-the-wall ideas take flight. Above all, encourage everyone to have fun!

In our research into companies that are considered to be particularly innovative, we found that certain core values repeatedly jumped out at us. One of the most common concerned respecting individuality and encouraging individual initiative. Companies in a variety of industries—from service providers such as American Express to technology concerns such as Hewlett-Packard and Sony to makers of consumer goods such as 3M and Philip Morris—all make it a point to clearly state their faith in their employees. They encourage everyone to contribute, or as Walt would say, they encourage everyone to dream. And from those vast stores of knowledge and creativity flow the innovative ideas that consistently keep them at the pinnacle of business success.

Other oft-stated core values are honesty, integrity, and an insistence on superior quality. IBM, Ford Motor, Boeing, General Electric, Merck, Motorola, and Procter & Gamble all espouse these upright notions, and all are among the greatest of American business success stories. It's fair to assume that an adherence to these basic beliefs has helped foster an atmosphere in which innovation can flourish.

And so it goes. Service to customers, hard work, continuous self-improvement, responsibility to society: These, too, are values that frequently carry great weight at many of the top companies. But don't mistake this as a laundry list from which you should choose your core values. While any or all of these may be relevant to your personal situation, the point to be made is that successful, innovative companies define what is important to them and then communicate those values to their employees. By encouraging everyone to live those values day to day, a secure, familiar atmosphere arises in which employees at every level feel comfortable breaking down traditional barriers and participating in a worthwhile way.

Innovation in terms of service is much of what defines Disney; indeed, stories of the company's employees going to great lengths to provide extraordinary service are common. One such story concerns a family that visited Disney World and stayed at the Disney hotel. The family included three little girls still young enough to take their teddy bears with them.

At the end of the first day, the family returned to their hotel room. There, seated around the table, were the three bears with cookies and milk placed before them. The little girls were delighted, of course, and the following evening they urged their parents to hurry back to the hotel. This time, the three bears were placed sitting up in bed "reading" Mickey Mouse books. One can imagine the joy this scene evoked in the youngsters. The third evening, the girls found their bears again at the table, but this time they were arranged as though playing cards!

The hotel cast member had truly taken to heart Walt's pronouncement that "visitors are our guests" and had come up with an innovative way to please the children and, by extension, their parents. At some shortsighted companies, management might have objected to spending extra money on cookies and milk. But at Disney, this welcoming gesture was a natural outgrowth of the company's unshakable commitment to customer service.

At Disney, providing innovative service extends into the business process arena as well. Some years ago, as we were walking through one of the parks, we noticed a kiosk for the Disney Vacation Club time-share condominiums. The first surprise came when we approached the kiosk operator; the lack of pressure was the complete opposite of our previous such experience at Lake Tahoe. There, after a high-pressure, two-hour sales pitch at a resort on the top of a mountain, we decided to forget the whole idea.

The Disney approach, we later learned, came about because Michael Eisner firmly vetoed any high-pressure sales tactics when he permitted the selling of time-share condominiums. So at Disney, we were told the purchase price right up front and were asked if we wanted to see the units. When we declined, the Disney cast member gave us what proved to be an informative and fun video that allowed us to tour the units at our leisure when we returned home. After our video tour, we were hooked.

Despite our excitement over buying a Disney product, we still dreaded the thought of closing, particularly a closing conducted by long distance. We both had memories of incomprehensible papers to read and sign, not to mention the mind-numbing and time-wasting interval spent sitting through the formalities. When we spoke to a Vacation Club cast member about our desire to buy and our fear of closing, he assured us that Disney had taken the pain out of the process. What an understatement! Within a few days, we were sent an accordion file with color-coded and tabbed sections, all clearly marked and explained in understandable, nonlegalese. Even the place for signatures was designated by its own color. Plus, there was another video. This one walked us through each step of the closing process. It was so simple, so attractive, and so enjoyable that we were almost tempted to buy a second unit just to repeat the experience!

In coming up with a successful process innovation, Disney basically reinvented the entire sales and closing procedure that has been standard in the real estate industry since time immemorial. The result for us and for every other Disney time-share condo buyer is fabulous service. Our experiences with the Disney Company reinforce the point that innovative companies begin to achieve real success by clearly stating their values and communicating them effectively to their staff. An inspiring, well-written vision statement is imperative in achieving full employee participation. However, writing such statements is not a simple task. Michael Snyder, the Vice President of Public Relations at Caldwell VanRiper, relayed to us his experience in this area.

> During Caldwell VanRiper's conversion to client-centered teams, we began the task of preparing a new vision statement of what the agency would reflect in the year 2002. The first two versions I prepared were rejected; they contained the content of an executive retreat we conducted in 1997 but did not reflect the spirit. After the second version was rejected, I had the opportunity to hear your presentation of "Dream, Believe, Dare, Do." Following this, I rewrote the statement as I really believed it ought to be. When the statement was later presented for the discussion, there was total silence. One of the first comments from a CVR executive was, "I want to work for this agency!"

Surging energy, great people, and a near-fanatical obsession with excellence will drive Caldwell VanRiper into national prominence. Top clients and superb talent will choose CVR because of its hot, progressive environment, where people don't care about what you look like or where you come from. At CVR, mediocrity is condemned. Superlative work sets the bar. Caldwell employees will celebrate life, achieving a positive balance between their professional and personal lives, fostered by the environment at CVR.

Client marketing problems are not just resolved at CVR, they are attacked and consumed by staffers, culminating in a reputation that transcends the definition of traditional communications. Experts and editors nationwide will eagerly seek out CVR staffers to tap into its communication mindset, which is akin to a band of well-trained, highly-armed guerillas storming a stronghold. Winning awards and achieving 30 percent growth annually are considered by staffers to be a byproduct of CVR's savage and unyielding commitment to brilliant solutions.

ALIGNING THE MISSION

The Disney Company is part of an industry that draws its strength from artistic talent, an intangible asset. At the same time, however, it must keep an eye on the very tangible bottom line. This is the kind of balancing act that concerns many businesses, not just those involved in providing entertainment. We help our clients to understand that missions clearly aligned with the overall values and beliefs of an organization produce hard-core business success. A visionary spirit can indeed rejuvenate a slumbering company. We have seen it happen often.

On one such occasion, we had the privilege of working with Jake Egan, the recently retired manager of the Product Testing Lab at the Whirlpool Refrigeration Technology Center. Jake was managing two pilot teams, the "testers" and the "technicians," in the organization's new cultural initiative. We asked both teams to individually contemplate their missions and draft statements that embodied their decisions.

The technician team's resulting statement seemed like motherhood and apple pie. Their generic sentences could easily have been pulled from any textbook or corporate mission statement poster. In a group meeting, we weighed the value of the statements against the following criteria: Does the mission address a means as well as an end? In other words, does it address how the mission should be accomplished as well as its desired result? Does it meet stakeholder needs and is there buy-in from the critical stakeholders? Will the mission be used as the constitution?

In the case of the technicians, the team members were unable to explore the depths of their true purpose and decide what values were important to them. We challenged them to go back and rethink their original draft, which they begrudgingly agreed to do.

After a few weeks, we reconvened. The leader of the technician team stood up and said, "When you asked us to go back and rethink our mission, we thought, 'What's the point? It's only a bunch of words.' But then we began discussing our values and listening to everyone's opinions on how we served our business partners."

The result was that when the team seriously answered the mission questions we posed in the earlier meeting, their values became crystallized and were evidenced by the inspired words in their new statement.

The important point to this story is that this team of hourly technicians had the motivation and conviction to reexamine critical aspects of how they do business without any supervision from management. This was a team that had fared poorly on all of the team categories, from goal-setting to conflict, by which they were benchmarked during their initial year of teaming. However, largely as a result of a visionary mission statement clearly aligned with company values, they made incredible advances within the next two years, perhaps more than any other team in the entire organization, while at the same time increasing the productivity of the entire department.

That's not to say that aligning team missions with the organizational vision is an easy task. It isn't. But with a little effort, you can come up with a system that allows you to integrate short-term activities with your longer-term vision. In tackling what we refer to as "policy deployment," you will realize a number of benefits, such as:

- Creating an established process for executing strategy.
- Increasing departmental cooperation.
- Giving your leadership a mechanism by which to understand key problem areas.
- Enabling quicker, more accurate feedback.

The concept of policy deployment involves setting up a structure that will allow your organization's overall objectives to cascade down through the various staff levels to the natural work group. We worked with a manufacturing team that used policy deployment to illustrate the process. (Figure 3-1 illustrates the policy deployment process for a client manufacturing team.)

Legend:
- ✓ Obvious Fit
- ? Potential Fit
- ! Area of Concern

Vision/Mission Key Points	Core Strengths				Values					Objectives				Stakeholders				
	Customer focus lab	Global engineering expertise	Rigorous design methodology	Name recognition	Teamwork	Innovation	Continuous learning	Customer focus	Respect	10x quality improvement	2% net material cost reduction	10% increase in team self-observation scores	Foster coworker development planning	End-product consumer	Internal process partners	Coworkers	Community	Company
Better quality	✓	✓	✓		✓	✓	?	✓		✓	!	?		✓		?	?	✓
Faster cycle times			✓		✓	✓	!			?	!	✓	!	?				✓
Lower costs	?	?	?			?	✓	!		✓	✓		!	✓				✓
Preferred consumer product	✓		✓	✓	✓			✓			!			✓		?		✓
Fun place to work					✓	?	✓						✓			✓	✓	?

FIGURE 3-1.   Policy deployment process for a client manufacturing process.

The organization's core strengths, values, objectives, and stakeholders are recorded on one axis. This represents a set of criteria by which the organization is measured. On the other axis, the key points of the mission or vision are recorded. The use of check marks (✓), question marks (?), and exclamation points (!) designates how well the mission or vision is aligned with the measurement criteria. In this example, the preferred consumer product vision is not supported by any of the objectives. One objective, the 2 percent net material cost reduction, could even be in conflict with the mission if the cost reductions compromise customer needs. The general manager of this organization said, "The value of policy deployment is not in the final output document; it is in the process that my staff and I went through to develop the document."

No company outdoes Disney in concern for its guests. But even Disney has occasionally made mistakes by failing to align short-term missions with overall beliefs and values. In the end, the company had to change its approach.

When its Pleasure Island attraction at Disney World opened with a jazz club, restaurants, and nightclubs, it was intended as a place for guests to go after other attractions had closed. The entertainment was still geared for the family, though, and even the nightclub atmosphere was relatively sedate. But in a reversal of Disney's usual policy, Pleasure Island was not gated; anyone could just walk right in. Problems arose almost immediately at this new entertainment complex. In the words of the company, "The fact that it was an 'ungated' attraction led to a number of security and guest-service issues."

Some guests were disturbed by the entertainment offered at the nightclubs, the company discovered, claiming it was too close to adult entertainment and not appropriate for their teenage children. It didn't take long for Disney to respond to the complaints. Within a year new leadership entered the scene and used the policy deployment matrix (Fig. 3-2) to highlight where the misalignment to the Disney measurement criteria had taken place. Once the misalignment was identified, a new vision of Pleasure Island was created to conform to the overall measurement criteria of the Disney theme park. The attraction was gated to control the entrances and promote safety; the entrance policy was changed to bar teenagers, with or without parents; nightclub entertainment was aimed at audiences between the ages of 22 and 45.

In this case, the Disney company briefly lost sight of the vision that had guided it for so many years, but in typical Disney fashion, it wasn't long before the mistake was rectified. Management's swift reaction saved the attraction from failure and turned it into a success.

You may not share all of Walt Disney's beliefs. He insisted, for example, that every production celebrate, nurture, and promote "wholesome American values." Cynicism was verboten at

Legend:
- ✓ Obvious Fit
- ? Potential Fit
- ! Area of Concern

Original Vision

Vision/Mission Key Points	Core Strengths				Values					Objectives				Stakeholders				
	Live entertainment	Variety of entertainment	Themed experience	Guest service	Risk-taking	Diversity	Originality	Creative imagination	Finest family entertainment	20% annual earnings/20% ROE	World's premiere entertainment company	Protect Disney name & franchise	Foster quality, imagination, & guest service	Family guest	Adult guests	Cast	Community	Company
Entertainment for families	✓ !		✓	✓					✓ !	?	✓	✓ !	✓	✓ !	✓			
Provide experiences to keep guest on property	✓	✓		✓				✓	✓ ?	?	✓	✓	✓	✓	✓	✓		✓
Provide nightclub atmosphere in the "Disney" way	✓	✓	✓	✓	✓	✓	✓	✓ !	✓ !		✓	✓ !		✓	✓		✓	
Non-gated to invite people to walk in		✓	✓ !	✓ !	✓ !	✓ !			? !			✓ !	✓ !		✓	!	? !	✓ !

New Vision

Vision/Mission Key Points	Live entertainment	Variety of entertainment	Themed experience	Guest service	Risk-taking	Diversity	Originality	Creative imagination	Finest family entertainment	20% annual earnings/20% ROE	World's premiere entertainment company	Protect Disney name & franchise	Foster quality, imagination, & guest service	Family guest	Adult guests	Cast	Community	Company
A party for adults	✓	✓	✓	✓	✓	✓	✓	✓	!	?	✓	!	✓	?	✓	?	?	?
Provide experiences to keep guest on property	✓	✓		✓				✓	?	?	✓	✓	✓	?	✓	✓		✓
Provide nightclub atmosphere for the 22- to 45-year-olds	?		?	✓	✓	!			!	?		?	✓		✓			
Gated to promote safety and entrance controls			✓											✓	✓	✓	✓	

Source: Disney University

FIGURE 3-2. Policy deployment process for realignment of Pleasure Island to the Disney criteria.

all levels. He could not and would not countenance a cynical attitude in his films, among his employees, or even from potential partner companies. Whatever your particular beliefs and values are, however, they should serve as a filter through which all decisions pass in order to test their validity and worthiness. The German writer Goethe observed that "when values are clear, laws are unnecessary. When values are not clear, laws are unenforceable."

Nor do we expect that most organizations will want to establish their own universities to train employees. Nevertheless, they can devise a process that will effectively communicate beliefs and values to employees, partners, and customers. In short, we are not suggesting that you embrace Disney's beliefs, values, and actions wholesale.

What we are urging is that you consider the Disney model and come to understand how devotion to your *own* core ideology can strengthen your organization. Having done that, you will be ready to enjoy the power that flows when everyone is engaged in living the same set of values and beliefs.

In the next two chapters, you will see how Disney extended the Believe concept to encompass both customers and suppliers.

Questions to Ask
- What are the values your company lives by?
- Who established those values?

  Customers?
  Employees?
  Managers?
  Directors?
  Stockholders?
  Founders?

- Are your personal values in conflict with those of the organization?
- What products and services does the organization provide?
- What methods does the organization apply to provide these products and services?

- For whom does the organization provide the products and services?
- Why does the organization exist?
- Are the actions and behaviors of your leaders consistent with the company's values?
- What mechanisms do you use to communicate your values to new employees?
- Does every department/team have a mission?
- Does the mission statement take advantage of the organization's core strengths?
- Does the mission create value for these stakeholders?
- Is each mission aligned with the overall company vision, values, and objectives?
- Do all departmental or work group goals, objectives, and tactics support the organization's vision and values?
- Do you refer to your mission when making decisions about products, services, customers, or coworkers?
- Do you share the mission statement with potential new hires?
- Can everyone, including the company janitor, articulate the organization's mission and values?
- What do your product development policies say about your values?
- Are all employees encouraged to be innovative in product, process, and service?
- Do your recent business decisions confirm your company's values?

Actions to Take
- Formalize your mission and values in a written statement to be used as the constitution.
- Encourage each department to prepare a policy-deployment exercise that aligns their mission with the organization's vision, values, core strengths, objectives, and stakeholder needs.

- Communicate all missions throughout the organization.
- Exhibit commitment to the organization's values through everyday actions.
- Evaluate all business decisions in light of the values.
- Conduct regular companywide meetings to reinforce the organizational vision and values.
- Hold a semiannual crazy-invention contest where *everyone* can submit off-the-wall product and service ideas. Reward winners and prototype their ideas.

A SHARED VISION

It isn't enough to corral a bunch of people and then expect them to function like a team. It needs much more than that. Every member's personal view of the project must be linked to the team's ultimate purpose so that a shared vision propels everyone's commitment.

"The way I saw my role," Whirlpool team leader Jerry McColgin remembers, "was one of bringing this group together, of making sure I was utilizing the talent that was there. I had an incredibly high level of competency within this group and my task was to harness this competency and to guide and direct the team."

One of the first steps Jerry undertook was to determine the personal values, the expectations, and the dreams of his group. As we facilitated this discussion during the team's Dream Retreat, spotting the similarities and striving to reinforce them was extremely rewarding. Jerry wanted to understand how the members saw the long-term value of their work and how strongly they believed in what they were doing. He attempted to paint a picture of what the team's work would involve. He pointed out that most major projects like theirs were given three to four years to bring to completion. Management expected the team to finish in a little over two years. In addition, the budget had been cut by a third.

McColgin, in consultation with us, decided that the best start would be to take the team off-site for a five-day retreat, a kick-off session. There, removed from outside distractions, this disparate group of people could begin to develop a true team spirit. We had created other teams for the company, but they were more traditional groups. As Jerry likes to say, he had "a whacko group of people from around the world who clearly weren't going to fit into a conventional business mold." Then, too, he had specific ends in mind: He wanted to establish a culture; he wanted the team to understand what his expectations were; and most of all, he was determined to create a 100 percent commitment from each team member.

NEVER A CUSTOMER, ALWAYS A GUEST

You don't build the product for yourself.
You need to know what the people want and build it for them.

WALT DISNEY

In an age when consumers all across the country bemoan the state of customer service, the Walt Disney Company is repeatedly hailed as a superior service provider, perhaps the best in the world. On the day Disneyland opened, Walt himself announced the theme park's motto: "At Disneyland, the visitors are our guests." Since then, the bar has continually been raised to new heights in the company's desire to delight its guests.

That visitors should be treated as guests is also a theme that emerges in nearly every movie Walt Disney made. The dwarfs welcome Snow White into their cottage, forest animals care for Bambi after his mother dies, the Banks family invite Mary Poppins into their home, and, of course, "Be Our Guest" is the title of one of the best-known songs from the 1991 film *Beauty and the Beast*. The guest motif is present in every corner of Disney, from the Magic Kingdom to Animal Kingdom.

Walt Disney knew instinctively what his visitors wanted. He didn't need to do expensive research into customer tastes because, as he once put it, his audience was "made up of my neighbors, people I know and meet everyday: folks I trade with, go to church with, vote with, compete in business with, help build and preserve a nation with."[9] Disney's understanding of his customer base coupled with his innate drive for perfection meant that audiences got more than they ever knew they wanted, whether in watching his films or visiting his theme park.

Know your guests, treat them honestly and with respect, and they will keep coming; that pretty well sums up what Walt Disney believed. The crowds that throng the Disney parks today, both here and abroad, testify to the enduring soundness of his belief. During the first week of November 1996, 793,000 people visited Disney's theme parks in the United States alone—and this in a week that didn't even include a school holiday.

Many of the companies we work with and others we have studied have wholeheartedly adopted Walt Disney's belief that customers should be treated as honored guests. Most of these companies are not in the service business per se; they have simply made it their business to provide excellent service. As you read their stories, you will see how an obsession with customers begets the kind of innovation that ultimately spells success.

HOW IMPORTANT ARE YOUR CUSTOMERS—REALLY?

You're probably wondering what companies don't try to please their customers? In reality, plenty. All too many companies seem to consider customers as nothing more than a necessary nuisance. Oh, they may say otherwise, but they don't deliver. If the road to hell is paved with good intentions, then the road to business failure is littered with placards proclaiming "the customer is always right."

A cavalier attitude toward customers is shortsighted in the extreme. The hard truth is that it costs five times more to attract a new customer than it does to keep an old one. What's more, a study conducted in 1994 by Bain Consulting in Boston concluded that a 5 percent increase in customer retention equals a 25 percent to 100 percent increase in profitability. A large number and a diverse grouping of the industries represented create the wide spread.

So if the payoffs are so great, why do companies fail when it comes to dealing with customers? The answer is *lack of leadership*. Without question, the CEO is the primary role model for every company value, and service is no exception. In an example of a leader who just didn't understand his responsibility, the CEO of a well-known rental car company was quoted as saying, "There's nothing more irritating than having the person next to you on a plane say, 'And what do you do for a living?' I used to be polite and tell them about my company, only to have my ear bent about the story of the dirty car in Chicago. Now when people tell me that story, I empathize with them and say, 'I know it's a lousy company. That's why I'm quitting.'"

Shocking, isn't it? Whatever happened to the customer focus of this CEO? Maybe he never had it.

More than a decade ago, Tom Peters told it like it is in his revolutionary book *Thriving on Chaos*:

> Each of us carries around a crippling disadvantage: we know and probably cherish our product. After all, we live with it day in and day out. But that blinds us to why the customer may hate it—or love it. Our customers see the product through an entirely different set of lenses. Education is not the answer; listening and adapting is.

The accuracy of Peters' words is borne out by an example with which we are particularly familiar. Bill's uncle, the owner of a newspaper distributorship in Chicago, had only an eighth-grade education and knew nothing about return on investment, asset turnover, or market segmentation analysis. He built his business on the simple premise that his customers paid him to deliver the paper at a reasonable time in readable condition. The customers' happiness was his primary concern. For three decades, Uncle Shorty never forgot the customer's perspective, even if that meant leaving the dinner table to attend to a complaint, which he did on many nights.

After 30 successful years as owner/operator, he sold the distributorship to people who went out of business within 10 years. How could the new owners go under when they had been handed a thriving business of long-standing? It's very simple: They did not attend to customer needs and solve customer problems. They made the mistake of operating the business like the monopoly it was, neglecting their home-delivery customers, and allowing service to the local retail stores to deteriorate.

The retailers' anger over shoddy service was compounded by the fact that they had no other choice but to buy from this distributor. Eventually, the growing number of complaints made directly to the Chicago newspaper publishers caused the distributor to lose their franchise.

All too many owners and CEOs are like the rental car executive or the newspaper distributor; they feel it is beneath them to concern themselves with dirty-car stories or late deliveries from their docks or doing whatever it takes to make a customer happy.

Although a "customers first" policy usually makes its way into most of the mission statements we've read, far too few companies really live those words. One of our clients, Illinois Power, is an exception, however.

In 1991, this company won the U.S. electric utility industry's top honor, The Edison Award, awarded by the Edison Electric Institute (EEI). Their efforts to better the company's relationship with customers and improve service through employee teamwork and empowerment had finally paid off. EEI Chairman, James Farrington, commented, "Illinois Power recognized that every customer is an individual, and that every individual has different needs and expectations. Through top-to-bottom internal initiatives and greater community involvement, IP is making sure those expectations are met or exceeded."

What really illustrated Illinois Power's commitment to its customer-first policy was the creation of a 24-hour customer center. Remember those Denny's commercials filling our living rooms with that serious voice echoing, "If a restaurant really loved you, it would never close"? A service organization is a different animal, though. Being there for customers 24 hours a day proves to us that Illinois Power's commitment to customers is more than just a line on the company mission statement.

TEST THE WELCOME MAT

One of the best ways to know for sure if customers really count is to evaluate how an organization deals with complaints. At one of our Dream Retreats, we learned from a participant whose daughter manages a Limited, Inc. store location in Arizona that the company will dismiss a store manager who receives three unresolved customer complaints.

At first, we were somewhat taken aback by the severity of this practice, but after a little research into the effects of customer complaints on the bottom line, we realized that the policy makes very good sense. The Technical Assistance Research Programs Corporation of Washington, D.C., which publishes statistics on customer complaints, has found that for every customer complaint that an organization receives, there are 26 other dissatisfied customers who will remain silent. Each of the 27 dissatisfied customers will tell 8 to 16 others about the experience, and 10 percent will tell more than 20 other potential customers. If you do the arithmetic, you will find that three complaints translate into more than 1000 potential customers hearing about the poor service a company provided. No company can afford to drag its feet when handling customer complaints.

We have been wowed many times by Disney's exceptional attention to guest problems and complaints. One example occurred when we were visiting Disney World with a group of clients.

After we had all checked into the hotel, we quickly departed for dinner. As we were riding along in one of the in-park buses that shuttle visitors around Disney World, the driver asked us how our rooms were. One of our clients mentioned that the faucet in his bar sink had an annoying drip, and he added that he hadn't had time yet to report it to maintenance.

"Sir, I'll take care of it for you," the driver assured him.

We didn't give it another thought, but when we got back from dinner about 10 o'clock, the faucet was fixed. And then, more impressive yet, shortly thereafter the driver showed up on his own time to make sure that the problem had been taken care of. This is the level of service you should aim for when you ask your employees to treat every customer like a guest in their own homes. The bus driver was truly committed to making the guest experience the best it could possibly be. That is service with a capital "S."

Like Disney, Dunn Hospitality, a client of ours that operates hotels throughout the Midwest, has a great reputation for handling complaints. Each Dunn employee has very specific responsibilities, but a complaint from a guest is owned by the employee who receives it, no matter whose area of responsibility the complaint involves. If you've ever complained to a front-desk employee about the absence of coffee at your morning seminar or a lack of toilet tissue in your room, the response at most hotels was probably something like "you should talk to the banquet manager" or "housekeeping takes care of that."

At a Dunn hotel, however, a complaint to anyone, from the front-desk manager to a bellhop to a housekeeper, will be solved by the person receiving your complaint. You can count on it.

THE DUNN HOSPITALITY CODES OF CONDUCT

We Work While Others Enjoy Their Stay
- We are open 365 days a year in all kinds of weather; convenience for our guests is our aim.
- We are here to make things easier for our guests.

We Create a Friendly Atmosphere
- Two musts: Practice a friendly smile; use friendly, courteous phrases.
- Maintain a neat, professional appearance.
- *Never* complain or comment on operating or personal problems.

We Give the Personal Touch
- Treat each guest as a special individual.
- One personal experience, good or bad, can make the greatest impression.
- Use the guest's name whenever possible.

We Know the Answers
- Any question, find the answer.
- Do not send guests in circles.
- Eliminate call transfers when possible.

We Know Our Roles
- All associates understand and strive to achieve their natural work group goals.

- Maintain uncompromising levels of cleanliness of our facilities.
- Record each incident of guest satisfaction.
- Every associate is empowered to resolve a problem of guest dissatisfaction and prevent a repeat occurrence.

We Make Our Facilities Clean and Safe
- Provide a safe environment for guests and associates.
- Notify the appropriate supervisor immediately of hazardous situations or injuries.
- Protect our assets. This is the responsibility of all associates.

We Are a Team
- We believe that our atmosphere needs to be friendly and informal.
- We take our jobs seriously, not ourselves. We create fun in our roles, which creates fun for our guests.
- We communicate openly; we do not promote barriers between people.

No recitation of extraordinary attention to customer complaints would be complete without a story about Nordstrom, the Seattle-based department store chain that wrote the book on making customers happy. As the following anecdote illustrates, the slightest dissatisfaction is taken quite seriously.

Bruce Nordstrom, cochairman, was leaving one of the stores on his way to a meeting when he overheard a woman say to her companion, "I've never been so disappointed in all my life." Nordstrom beckoned to a sales associate and asked her to find out why the woman was disappointed. The sales associate followed the two women out to the street and politely asked what had happened to them in the store.

The ladies laughingly explained, "It's not the store. The problem is that we have champagne taste on a beer budget. We fell in love with a dress and it's way too expensive for us."

Now, at virtually every other department store in the world, we would bet that the sales associate would have made a mildly sympathetic comment and wished the ladies a good day. But not at Nordstrom. This associate escorted the two back into the store to a department where they each bought two dresses that cost less than the original find.

Equally important was what happened when Bruce Nordstrom returned from his meeting: He made a point of finding the sales associate to ask about the two customers. By indicating his interest in the outcome, the top man sent the employee a strong signal that service is of paramount importance to the Nordstrom's of Seattle.

SOLVING CUSTOMER PROBLEMS SPARKS INNOVATION

Customer service is more than just taking care of customer-expressed needs and demands. Companies must also investigate and solve customer problems in the areas of product, process, and service. Before that can happen, however, an organization's leadership has to create an environment that encourages everyone to listen to customer problems and try to accomplish the impossible. It takes effort to do this well.

One company that does it extremely well is Four Seasons Hotels. Known throughout the world as a first-class chain, Four Seasons is very sensitive to the needs and problems of its guests, as an incident at the New York hotel amply illustrates.

Just as a guest was being whisked away in a cab, the door-man noticed that the man's briefcase was lying by the curb. Checking inside the briefcase, the doorman located the phone number of the man's firm. He called the guest's secretary and told her what had happened.

"He's on his way to a very urgent meeting in Boston," she said, "and I'm sure he needs the papers in his briefcase."

Without hesitation, the doorman asked for the guest's flight number and volunteered to take the briefcase to him at the airport before he departed. With a substitute on duty, the doorman jumped into a cab and raced to the airport, but he was delayed in traffic and arrived too late.

The doorman again called the secretary, who thanked him for his efforts while expressing regret over the whole situation. But the doorman told her not to worry because he had just purchased a ticket on the next shuttle to Boston and would personally deliver the briefcase to the man at this meeting. Without asking anyone's approval, the doorman flew to Boston and saved the day!

In most companies, one of two scenarios would happen next. Either the doorman would be a hero for solving the guest's problem, or he would be fired for failing to gain the appropriate approvals before flying off to Boston. At the Four Seasons, he was neither a hero nor a scapegoat, because extraordinary service is all in a day's work. Every Four Seasons employee is expected to do whatever it takes to ensure that each guest has a positive and memorable experience. The environment demands it.

Problem-solving is so ingrained, in fact, that Four Seasons employees have been known to jump into action long before an individual has become a guest, as we discovered when working with the CEO of a large consulting firm in Chicago.

In preparation for a major retreat where partners from around the world would be in attendance, we suggested using a hotel at the airport to conserve expenses. But the CEO insisted on using the Four Seasons, and he explained his preference by relating an extraordinary tale about the hotel's downtown location.

It seems that the CEO was a board member at a Chicago museum that enlisted Nancy Reagan as the featured speaker at its fund-raising event. The CEO was expected to join other board members in the receiving line to greet the then First Lady. Arriving at the Four Seasons after a hectic day at the office, he noticed that people entering the grand ballroom were in formal attire. Not having checked his invitation for several weeks, he had forgotten that this was a black-tie event.

There he was in his business suit with no time to go home and change. As he stood in the lobby contemplating what he should do, the concierge, seeing the look of consternation on his face, approached him and asked, "Is there anything I can do for you, sir?" After the CEO explained his dilemma, the concierge volunteered, "One of the waiters is off today, and I know he would not mind if you wore his tuxedo."

When the two men went to the locker room, they found a clean shirt but the tuxedo had been taken to the cleaners. The CEO thanked the concierge for his trouble, but the concierge refused to give up. "You can wear my tuxedo!" he offered as he began to disrobe.

Not deterred by the fact that he was two sizes larger than the CEO, the concierge attempted to staple the arms and legs to make them look presentable. And when that didn't work, the concierge called the hotel tailor who came immediately and fixed the tuxedo on the spot.

The CEO took his place in the receiving line and no one was the wiser!

To top the whole thing off, when he returned from the event, he found that his business suit had been pressed and hung neatly on a hanger. The CEO, wishing to express his gratitude, began pulling out all the cash in his pocket plus his checkbook. But the concierge refused to accept any payment, insisting that he had only been doing his job, which was to serve the guests and solve their problems.

"But I'm not even a guest," the CEO said. "I just walked in off the street." To which the concierge replied, "Well, maybe someday you will be."

The CEO was sold on Four Seasons, of course, and decided that the honored guest at the first dinner of the retreat would be that concierge. The CEO presented him with a brass clock, which he graciously accepted while reiterating, "I was only doing my job."

Another well-known name in the hospitality business with an equally well-known reputation for providing stellar service is Marriott International. In our work with one of the Marriott hotels, we got an immediate sense of the company's motto: "Go beyond." Go beyond what your customers expect, and surprise them with your ability to solve their problems. An incident at one of the company's smaller hotels outside Seattle illustrates how this value is lived every day at Marriott.

A guest checked into the hotel and began to prepare for the first big speech of her career. When she unpacked her laptop computer to retrieve her speech, she realized that she had forgotten to bring the computer cord and the battery. The hotel management quickly located compatible replacements, but this guest's problems were just beginning.

As she booted up the machine, her hard drive crashed. Any computer user can imagine her panic. But once again, the hotel came to her rescue by allowing her to use a desk and a computer in the hotel's accounting office. Staff members coached her on using the unfamiliar machine and then enlisted other employees to listen to the guest rehearse her speech. In a final gesture of superior service, they all showed up for the big event, where she was enthusiastically received by her audience.

Innovative problem-solving has given rise to centuries' worth of inventions and products, most of which we take for granted and many of which we would be hard-pressed to do without. Consider the ubiquitous Post-it™ Notes, those sticky little squares of paper that decorate every imaginable surface in homes and offices across the land.

No wild-eyed inventor came up with the notion in a dingy little basement workshop. Rather, the product came about as the result of a problem that a 3M employee recognized and solved.

This particular employee, who happened to be a member of his church choir, was annoyed that he often lost his place in the hymnal. One day at work, a solution dawned on him. He experimented with some glue that had been shelved because of its inferior bonding qualities. Not strong enough to serve its intended purpose, it turned out to be just right for holding little yellow squares in place on a hymnal page.

What began as the solution to an individual problem turned into a wildly successful and profitable product line.

Customer problems are sometimes difficult to discern because they surface only under certain conditions or situations. Nevertheless, problems are certainly there for the finding. And while your customers' problems may not open the door to a Post-it Note gold mine, they can offer you the chance to provide the kind of customer service that will set your organization apart from the crowd.

SUPERIOR PROCESS EQUALS
SUPERIOR SERVICE

We continually stress that innovation is needed in every process, not just in products and services. Nowhere is the acceptance of that idea more urgent than at the many companies that deal directly with the consumer market. How many of them have an adequate—not extraordinary, mind you, just adequate—process in place for providing customer service? Few, indeed, if we are to judge by the inordinate amounts of time that most of us waste on the phone waiting for a human voice to respond to a need, or, for that matter, to rescue us from the annoying music we are forced to listen to.

In an effort to help the Mead Johnson Nutritional division of Bristol-Myers Squibb improve its customer service early this decade, we facilitated a complaint analysis team. The team was given responsibility for reengineering the customer service process, specifically for figuring out how to cut the time that callers were kept on hold. At Mead Johnson, mothers might call in because their children are sick and they have questions about the baby formula they are using. No mother with a sick child has the time or the patience to hang on the phone; she needs and often demands immediate assistance.

A surprising statistic that surfaced from the team's work was that a majority of the calls came during the lunch hour. It was obvious that employee lunch hours needed to be staggered, with some taking an earlier lunch, others going later. This simple solution considerably cut the time callers had to spend on hold.

Clearly, innovation in process is alive and well in some organizations. As Dr. William Cross, vice president at Mead Johnson, says,

> We have tried very hard to find out how we are meeting our customers' needs and where we need to improve. Putting all the emphasis on the customer's needs and continually improving how we meet those needs—that's how we have been able to eliminate waste from our systems.

Another of our clients, a builder of prefab houses, has found an unusual way to bring his customers into the process.

From the initial step of signing the agreement and on through the entire construction process, photographs are taken to record events. Furthermore, a photograph of the family is attached to the work order. As construction proceeds, from digging the foundation to hanging the front door, the camera is present to shoot pictures for and with the family. Besides making the home seem real to the buyers, it also helps to personalize the project for the workers. They are not just building Work Order No. 48, they are building a home for a family they have come to know. Such face-to-face interaction motivates the workers to do a good job and to take pride in their efforts.

In our experience, large manufacturing companies often rank customer problem solving far down on their list of priorities. Senior management, in many instances, believes that middle managers should devote all their energies to strategy, systems, and training issues. Most plant managers seem to be trapped in a world of direct supervision and paperwork.

Besides allotting scant time to customer interaction, plant managers also have little time for quality function deployment, a method of incorporating the "voice" of the customer into the manufacturing process. We urge managers in manufacturing companies to follow Walt Disney's example, as mentioned in Chapter 3, and recognize situations in which one value should take precedence over another. Spend at least 30 percent of your time on customer needs and problem solving.

However, before a company can hope to excel with innovative product, service, or process, it must know its market. Perhaps most disturbing to us is that the majority of organizations know neither what customers want nor what their problems are. To demonstrate this point, we frequently ask the participants in our workshops to list the three most important features or services needed at a retreat or seminar. The number one answer is the availability of telephones. The number two and three answers relate to the location of the restrooms and easy access to the coffeepots. But when we ask hotel managers what three things attract business customers to their hotels, they usually say, "our great food, ample parking, and atmosphere." What's more, this phenomenon is not unique to the hotel industry. From computers to automobiles to restaurants, we have found the same story. These industries do not know their customers' problems.

Even Disney has made mistakes when entering new markets. EuroDisney, the 4800-acre theme park built outside Paris, got a lot of press when it stumbled badly after its 1992 opening. Disney erred by opening a park suitable for an American audience in a country whose culture differed from ours in many respects. For example, originally, no wine was served in the park. No wine? In France? The French have never accepted American culture with wholehearted enthusiasm to begin with, and they sourly regarded EuroDisney as just another example of Yankee imperialism.

Disney soon made changes, however, and today the park, which was renamed Disneyland Paris a couple of years ago, is beginning to rank with the other theme parks in popularity and in revenues. Mistakes can indeed be a valuable learning tool if a company ferrets out the causes and then uses the feedback to design appropriate solutions.

GETTING YOUR COMPANY ON TRACK

From the beginning, Walt Disney instilled his organization with the idea that every moment should be magical for its guests. Since nothing is more important at Disney, the company makes sure every employee buys into that belief through its formal training programs at Disney University. New recruits are immediately made to feel that they can play a significant role and be a part of something with a higher purpose.

In most organizations, however, the people who have the primary contact with the customer usually are the least educated, least trained, least respected, and have the least input regarding the direction of the company. And unfortunately, too many customer service training programs deal only with how to smile and greet the customer, leaving service providers without a clue about how to solve a problem. Treating customers with respect and communicating in a pleasant manner are indeed important, but smiles alone will not improve customer service.

If your organization is among the ranks of the clueless, do the following two things well, and listen for favorable customer response:

1. *Become a customer-problem solver.*   We are convinced that the quality of orientation at most companies would have to increase tenfold to reach the "pathetic" level. Orientation for frontline workers usually consists of how to fill in the time card and how to complete an order form. In rare cases, a 30-minute session on how to talk to a customer is added. Organizations then disguise unskilled frontline employees by hanging a sign on them that reads, TRAINEE. What that really means is, "Don't expect me to know anything; I'm trying to figure out what goes on here too."

Within the first week of employment, your frontline coworkers should be able to answer the following questions with assurance:

- What products and services do we provide? It is not a matter of being able to point to the catalog and describe the products, but rather of knowing how to solve the problems and fill the needs of the customers.
- What are the organization's vision and values?
- What is the mission for my department?
- Who are our competitors and what is our competitive advantage?
- To whom do I turn for assistance with a problem I cannot solve?

2. *Gain customer feedback.*   Customer perceptions are very powerful and often become reality. Therefore, every system in the organization must be evaluated through customers' eyes. Two critical questions to ask yourself are:

- What is the level of ease of doing business with our organization?
- What do we consider to be exceptional service?

Many customer feedback tools, such as surveys and focus groups, require a considerable investment of people, time, and money to put in place. Evaluate your budget to ensure that you are not skimping on these critical activities. Recognize also that you have a wealth of customer information at your fingertips just waiting to be tapped. Consider anyone who has customer contact as a barometer for measuring both positive and negative customer perceptions. Ask accounting clerks and order entry clerks alike to call customers and ask the simple question, "How did we do on that delivery last week?"

Simple efforts like these let your customers know that you care about their experiences. They also send a clear message to employees about the value of customer perceptions.

THE POSITIVE AND NEGATIVE POWER OF PERCEPTION

The Physics Department at San Jose State University prided itself on having a freshman physics class that was so difficult that 50 percent of the students routinely flunked out of or dropped the class. One semester, a professor decided to do an experiment. In the first of two identical classes, he stated during his opening lecture that 50 percent of the students would flunk or drop out. In his second class, he stated that the normal flunk-out rate was 50 percent, but in looking through the students' transcripts, he was astounded to see that everyone in this class had an exceptional aptitude in math and science.

You can probably guess the results. In the first class, 50 percent of the students dropped out or flunked. In the second class, every student passed with a grade of C or better.

The point of this story is that perceptions really do become reality.

PERCEPTION BECOMES A GRIM REALITY

The power of perception takes on a strangely disturbing cast in this story of a railroad worker in California.

The man was sent to check on some freight in a refrigerated boxcar. While inside the car, the doors shut accidentally, trapping him inside. When the man failed to check in at the end of the shift, a coworker found him dead in the boxcar. The following words were written on the walls: "No one is hearing my cries for help. My hands and feet are getting colder. I don't know how much longer I can last."

The eerie fact of this story is that the boxcar had been side-lined on a spur because its refrigeration unit was not working. The temperature outside was in the eighties, and although the temperature in the boxcar was slightly lower, it was nowhere near freezing. There was also plenty of air for the man to breathe.

So what happened? His perception of freezing to death was so strong that it became reality.

Plumbing & Industrial Supply has a heightened understanding of customer perceptions and a firm set of long-term beliefs. Thus, when an elderly gentleman came to the retail counter area of the company one day, he received a reception that is, we're sad to say, not typical of most businesses.

The apparently lonely old fellow asked a lot of general questions and didn't seem as if he were a serious buyer. "My initial reaction," said the counter attendant, "was to return to my other duties of stocking shelves and processing orders. However, having just attended a three-day retreat in which we talked about treating the customer as if he were a guest in our own homes, I continued to converse with the man for about two hours."

The following day, this seemingly unlikely customer returned to place a $500 order. What's more, he related that he had told his sons, who were taking over his construction business, about the fine hospitality he had received the day before. He assured the counter attendant that his company looked forward to a long-term business relationship with Plumbing & Industrial Supply!

Walt Disney would have appreciated the counter attendant's story, for he always focused special attention on those who dealt directly with theme park visitors—the ticket takers, the waiters, the security officers, and the people who operated the rides and other attractions. That's because he recognized that those people were the ones who made the invaluable direct impression on the Disney guests.

If you have ever visited one of the Disney theme parks, chances are that you've had a cast member stop to chat with you and ask which attractions you've been on, whether you need anything, if you're having a good time, and so forth. In other words, have they treated their guests like any good host would?

To ensure that his frontline cast members would always deliver superior and pleasing service to the guests, Walt Disney went out of his way to make sure that employees were satisfied with their jobs and with the company. No one had to tell Walt that workers who are happy take pride in their work and do it well.

Front line equals bottom line is still an accepted rule at the Disney company.

Walt also recognized that teamwork is a necessary component of the good show. Many of our clients are utilizing empowered teams and reaping the benefits of more efficient and effective performance. Guests may come first, but cast members are not far behind, as you will see in the chapter that follows.

Questions to Ask
- Do you know your "guests"?
- Are your employees empowered to solve customer problems?
- Do you view your front line as your bottom line?
- What special training do your frontline people receive?
- What is the turnover rate among your frontline staff?

Actions to Take
- Ask coworkers to experience how the customer is being treated in your organization.
- Recognize and reward outstanding customer service.
- Establish a mechanism for customers to comment on how they've been treated by coworkers.
- Encourage coworkers to regularly visit customers to discuss customer problems and dreams.
- Pay a little more than the going scale for frontline coworkers.
- Encourage every coworker to call two to three customers each week to ask, "How are we doing?"
- Recruit people who like people.

AN INNOVATIVE GROUP

You can't expect to have a group of 35 people without a few among them exhibiting a "show me" attitude. "I was trying to establish a culture that was strange to them—a departure from the norm that they had always worked in," Whirlpool's McColgin asserts. Yet in the end, the cohesion of the team and the prevalent belief in the goals that were set proved the skeptics wrong.

What really excited everyone was the fact that they were members of an innovative group. They were approaching their jobs in a way they had never done before. McColgin was determined that everyone would participate. He wanted, as he put it, to "get people's hearts into it, get them to understand the goals, so that they could support them."

To achieve that end, McColgin asked each team member specifically what he or she wanted to get out of the project. Many people answered by saying that they felt they were in a pioneering team and they hoped to learn enough to be able to participate in similar projects in the future. One man made a comment that he hoped to learn about functions outside his own specialty; he wanted to get a feel for other people's work. As we were planning to set up cross-functional subteams, he got his wish.

Jerry pointed out to his team that all through their work, they had to bear in mind not the product and its costs alone but also the customers and the suppliers. The big advantage that the team brought to the project was its international character. The members from Brazil or India or any other of the countries represented were, in effect, wearing two hats. Professionally, they were engineers or marketing people, but back home they were also customers, who were now sitting right in the room with Whirlpool's American employees. They knew what the needs of their own people were.

Focus groups were also used in this international market to determine customer wants. Several participants said that they wanted ice trays. Corrosion resistance was an issue in tropical regions; a quiet motor was important in countries where the refrigerator often stood in the living room; and the number of kilowatts per hour—the cost of the electricity—was a major factor in other areas.

All this research helped the team's designers and engineers to meet customer requirements and save money.

ALL FOR ONE
AND ONE FOR ALL

Many hands, and hearts, and minds generally contribute to anyone's notable achievements.[10]

WALT DISNEY

He was renowned for his creativity and superior craftsmanship and was successful beyond compare, yet even the great Walt Disney did not presume to be able to accomplish his goals without the contributions of a well-coordinated group working alongside him. "I don't propose to be an authority on anything at all," he once explained. "I follow the opinions of ordinary people I meet, and I take pride in the close-knit teamwork of my organization."[11]

That Walt Disney so readily acknowledged the value of collaboration is a measure of his greatness—or perhaps a cause of it. In any event, his belief in the team concept was such that he promoted it both in his films and throughout his company. In fact, teamwork is a crucial element underpinning the Disney "be our guest" philosophy: To wit, exceeding guests' expectations requires a well-rehearsed cast, with every member playing a significant role.

In the area of feature animation, the Disney organization taps the collective power of its workforce by using a long-standing process for determining the value of various concepts for production. As a first step, the president and vice president of feature animation, along with CEO Michael Eisner and

Roy E. Disney, vice-chairman of the board, discuss ideas from several sources to decide which to pursue.

As the project moves along, directors, art directors, and the head of background production all join in the give-and-take of planning. The dialogue eventually produces a consensus, and company insiders insist that no one ever asserts an attitude of possessiveness. The teamwork continues throughout the long process of animation, camera work, adding sound, and editing until, at last, the film is ready for release.

References to teamwork also are sprinkled throughout Disney films, but none better illustrates Walt's belief in the value of collaboration than *Snow White and the Seven Dwarfs*. For many of us, those seven distinctive little fellows—Happy, Sleepy, Doc, Bashful, Sneezy (originally named Jumpy), Grumpy, and Dopey—are childhood friends. Each was carefully drawn with his own distinguishing characteristics, yet we remember them first and foremost as a team, always going off to work each morning whistling a happy tune. Walt purposely made the notion of cooperative endeavor an integral part of that script, with the dwarfs illustrating how different talents and personalities can be brought together to accomplish shared goals.

Many of the companies we work with have become convinced, like Walt Disney, that it takes a multifunctional team to produce the best possible show. They are using teams in their everyday operations and deriving benefits—such as enhanced problem solving—that help to ensure long-term success. Look to these examples to guide your organization in tapping the latent power of its collective wisdom.

A COMMON FOCUS IS ESSENTIAL

For many of us, the word "team" conjures up images of a football field or memories of the Little League games we played during our school years. In sports, teams have always aroused emotions of intense loyalty and enthusiastic support. By adopting the team concept, we can transport this loyalty, enthusiasm, and commitment associated with the playing field to the business arena. What's more, companies find that when management successfully brings together a diverse, multitalented group of employees to work together in a complementary fashion, the team members both challenge and support one another in a winning synergy that constantly improves the organization.

But to back up a bit, it's important to lay the preliminary groundwork for successful teaming, namely, to instill a shared sense of purpose and commitment to the team.

At Disney, team commitment is fostered in many ways, including the storytelling technique described in Chapter 2. And on movie projects, where teamwork is essential, Disney deviates from the norm in that collaboration is not just a one-time thing, with the participants gathered for one particular film. Many of the teammates are staff members who have worked together before. This is especially true when it comes to animated films, which demand special, well-honed skills. Most important, all the participants have been trained in Disney traditions. Knowing exactly what is expected of them and what the company stands for further strengthens the team spirit.

Besides in-house training, another way to develop a common focus is through a mission statement. A written statement of a team's mission and goals is a necessity to communicate the direction to all team members.

Teams can be crippled by the corporate policy manual, which often distracts them from accomplishing their mission. Any new employee—and many well-seasoned ones—would have trouble absorbing all the policy regulations that these weighty tomes contain. Moreover, burying any kind of mission statement inside what is bound to be a deadly dull recitation of rules and regulations virtually guarantees that it will be overlooked or quickly forgotten.

Not long ago, we were chatting about policy manuals with a well-known business leader who told us the following story. Years ago, as a new, young department head, he was approached by an old-timer who offered to get him a copy of the company's newly prepared, 150-page policy manual. The young man thanked him, weighed the policy statement book in his right hand, and then sat down at his typewriter and came up with a new version. It read: "Work hard, be clever, have fun, use good judgment." In effect, this insightful new employee reduced 150 pages of ponderous prose to a mere nine words that said pretty much the same thing.

We recommend that our clients follow his lead and keep brevity and clarity in mind when setting policy. Your goal should be to enable the kind of creative environment in which problems are solved, productivity is increased, and teams are empowered. Teams that are burdened by excessive rules and procedures are likely to spend an inordinate amount of time dealing with internal functional issues and not solving customer problems. Creativity will most certainly be stifled.

BRINGING THE MISSION TO LIFE

The best way to give a mission statement meaning is to establish multifunctional teams to carry out the organizational values. Many teams manage to craft mission statements that sound wonderful, but as we mentioned in the preceding chapter, they are often little more than an exercise with no real substance. When we begin working with teams, we point out that the statements are only as good as their execution.

Once a team's mission is developed and all members have confirmed their buy-in, the team can solve problems quicker and institute changes more effectively than can a handful of loners working on their own. As we have witnessed with our clients, bringing people together in cross-functional teams often sparks a flurry of new ideas that, in turn, produce solutions to problems. Because such teams constantly draw on the diverse experiences and opinions of a number of people from across the organization, they are better able to look at the company as a whole and suggest integrated product, service, and process improvements. In short, multifunctional teams are much better suited to rethinking the old and leading the way to the new.

In general, an organization's top management must formally lay the groundwork and provide the impetus for a team-based structure, although we have run across teams that seem to form spontaneously, inspired, perhaps, by common sense. Just such an example drew our attention recently at an east-coast utility.

We have done consulting work for many utility companies, usually auditing on a management level. In the process, we look at the cost of materials and how trucks are purchased. Used sometimes in maintenance work, sometimes in an emergency, utility trucks are a familiar sight on suburban streets and country roads. They constitute a major investment for utility companies. Traditionally, whether the buying is done by a group in the corporate structure or, as sometimes happens, by a special purchasing group, the responsibility has always rested in the hands of white-collar executive personnel. The work crews that operate from the trucks and the people who drive and maintain them have nothing to do with acquiring them.

At our east-coast client, the vice president in charge of materials was new on the job, having spent many years as a purchasing manager for an airline company. When we asked him how he went about buying needed supplies, his honesty and candor were both refreshing and instructive. He readily admitted that he didn't know anything about utility trucks, even though he was charged with buying hundreds of them. So what did he do?

"I got a group of line workers together," he said, "the people who were using the trucks, plus people from purchasing and an accountant, and I said to them, 'Go into a room and don't come out until you can give me the specs for a truck.' And you know what? We saved a ton of money, and for the first time ever, the line workers were really pleased with equipment we got for them."

Contrast that story with one we heard from a group of line workers at another utility. The purchasing department bought trucks without any consultation with line workers, who were forced to come up with their own solution: "When we get a new truck in," they told us, "we cut things off of it and weld things onto it. In two or three weeks, we have that truck the way we want it."

Innovative? Absolutely. Efficient? No way! But this is exactly the kind of thing that happens when management is wedded to the oft-heard principle, "That's the way we've always done things here." Through either hubris or inertia, outmoded and costly methods of operation remain in place year after year, leader after leader.

But this need not be so. Any manager can imitate the innovative vice president at the first utility who organized a multifunctional group of people to work together to find the best possible solution to a problem. Rather than following an inefficient and imprudent practice, however "standard," and ordering a fleet of expensive trucks or some other high-priced item, a manager can take the initiative to change any wrong-headed procedure. But taking that initiative often means bringing the frontline people into the process, people who know what is needed, as in the case of the utility that acquired trucks meeting workers' needs. At the same time, this team saved the company a lot of money, planning well in advance of the purchase and coming in well under budget.

When properly structured, teams can improve everything from the bottom line to employee satisfaction with the job. In fact, much of the research we see suggests that in a tight market for the top-notch recruits in technology, production, and other fields that demand both high intelligence and high levels of skills, people are attracted to jobs with the most expansive descriptions and opportunities for advancement. Salary is important, to be sure, but it is often not the first criterion that the best people have in mind when they begin evaluating job possibilities or offers. As R. S. Dreyer writes in a recent article for *Supervision* magazine, people work not only for the salary, but also "for the satisfaction they derive from accomplishment. They work to be part of a team...[and] for the feeling of pride they get out of being employed by a fine organization."

In our work with the Mead Johnson Nutritional Division of Bristol-Myers Squibb, for example, we found confirmation of the greater sense people derive from working as members of a successful team. One line attendant, a production line employee whose job it is to make sure that the line doesn't jam up, told us her story about working at a plant that produces infant formula. This employee was responsible for picking up overturned bottles. It's a bit like being a traffic cop, except that watching the line all day can be monotonous and boring. When she was put on a team, however, her whole attitude about the job changed.

Here's how she explained it: "Before I joined the team, I was always proud to say that I worked for Bristol-Myers, but when asked what my specific job was, I usually changed the subject. The truth was that I was embarrassed to say I was a line attendant. Now it's different; I tell anyone who asks that I'm a member of a team that is responsible for making the best quality product at the most affordable cost for mothers and babies throughout the world."

No longer just a lone worker in a monotonous job, this woman became part of a multifunctional team that met with management in an effort to improve quality and productivity. Having been made to feel that her work and her opinions mattered, she was able to take pride in her new role and to exhibit striking enthusiasm, loyalty, and commitment to the team.

TOPPLING HIERARCHICAL BARRIERS

Although no organization can function without a certain degree of hierarchy (someone must be in charge), every company should look at how well its hierarchy performs and periodically question its purpose. Some stratification is vital to the smooth functioning of any business, but too much can, and probably will, kill initiative, smother innovation, and lead to a deadening of the spirit throughout the organization.

Consider organizing teams around processes. If visitors were to have visited EPCOT's METLife exhibit several years ago, they would have come in contact with many different departments: merchandising, food service, attractions, maintenance, and horticulture. To the guest, the barriers to providing service were invisible. But cast members recognized problems in delivering the great service we have come to expect. For example, whose job was it to clean up the Body Wars attraction if someone got sick? Was it maintenance or attractions? So they decided to organize around the process. Everyone associated with the attraction now is a member of one team. Their job is to make sure the guest has a pleasant and memorable experience. The whole team is focused on the guest experience and not on who is responsible for what.

Restructuring an organization's operations around teams goes a long way toward breaking down rigid managerial barriers. What results is a win-win situation. Lower-level employees feel empowered when they are encouraged to voice opinions and make suggestions in a group that includes a manager. In turn, the organization derives the enormous benefit of being able to draw from a valuable source of new ideas and knowledge. The hierarchy remains, but the distance between managers and employees is diminished.

The Disney Company well understands that worthwhile suggestions can be lost because employees will hesitate to make them in a normal hierarchical business atmosphere. That's why the Gong Show exists. But in addition to giving employees specific venues for making suggestions, top Disney executives go out of their way to solicit advice from staff members, those frontline people who hear guests' comments and see their reactions.

A few years ago, for example, Michael Eisner was walking through an EPCOT computer technology exhibit called "Innoventions." It was anything but innovative. There was nothing particularly imaginative or inspiring about the technology displays, and the CEO was not pleased with it. So he stopped and asked some of the greeters at the exhibit if they had any ideas about how to liven it up. Told that another cast member by the name of Mike Goames talked a lot about what needed to be done to brighten up the place, the CEO approached him to ask for some ideas. Impressed by what Goames had to say, Eisner asked him to detail his suggestions in a memo. (Goames suggested that the exhibit should look more like a technical trade fair, showcasing new technologies and experimental things like wrist telephones.)

We recently told this story about Eisner and Goames at a public seminar where two employees of the local Disney retail store were in attendance. After the seminar, they approached us and one of them, the store manager, remarked, "Michael Eisner has never been in our store. But if he ever does visit, I really believe that he would want to hear our ideas. That's just the culture at Disney. The company respects the ideas from all cast members, regardless of their level in the organization."

Few companies seem willing or able to trust and empower employees to quite the extent we have witnessed at Disney. The Disney approach stems, we believe, from a long history of teamwork and cooperation between management and employees that dates back to the way Walt managed the company in the early days. In fact, the Goames incident is reminiscent of the story recounted in the opening chapter in which Walt added fireflies to his Disneyland Caribbean attraction in response to the suggestion of a construction worker at the park.

An astonishing indication of the depth of employee trust and empowerment at Disney is the fact that its customer service representatives, the people who take the tickets at the theme park entrances, have $500,000 in tickets and cash at their disposal to give out to guests who lose or forget their tickets, run out of money with which to get home, or encounter any other problem that merits attention. That's an extraordinary sum of money to place at the discretion of employees, but Disney obviously trusts these empowered cast members to use sound judgment.

What's more, it's noteworthy because of what it says about how Disney has eliminated turf barriers. How many accounting departments would allow a frontline worker to have such power and latitude? The point is that at Disney no single department calls the shots for any other.

FACTORS IN SUCCESSFUL
TEAM BUILDING

Not every team experience is going to be a success, of course. There are those who complain that when they introduced the team concept in their companies, it didn't work. But when the team approach fails, there is usually a good reason for it.

To begin with, setting up teams is not always easy. Much depends on the selection of a leader, who will play a pivotal role in determining the results. This individual has an enormous responsibility to set the tone for the team, both through personal attributes and through the choice of individual team members. He or she must be capable of exercising firm and fair leadership that respects each member's personal values and understands the role each individual plays. A successful leader will establish and manage a climate that encourages creativity while keeping team members on track to accomplish assigned goals. Finding such a person takes thoughtful consideration, but we've yet to encounter a company without qualified candidates.

The composition of the rest of the team is a major factor in its success or failure too. You must first determine all the stakeholders on a particular project, then move to find the best representative of each of the needed skill sets. And as basic as it sounds, we always urge our clients to consider the personalities of potential members. Inveterate pessimists should be avoided. Management must also make sure to include detail-oriented people as well as big-picture thinkers. You don't want to end up with a group in which everyone looks at the end result but no one is paying attention to all the little things that will make it happen. Diversity is important, but in the end, it's all about synergy, balance, and raising the bar for one another.

How does a leader create an environment in which team members can thrive? First of all, he or she must encourage the free flow of ideas by letting team members know that no idea is too ridiculous. It stands to reason that when innovation is the goal, radical premises are to be encouraged, not squelched. Group discussion and analysis can often transform a seemingly off-the-wall notion into a sensible and usable tool.

Group discussion can also turn an entire team around if it's heading off in a wrong direction, especially if the team leader loses touch with the team and their problems. Such is the case of a person we'll call John, one of 24 team leaders at a manufacturing company we worked with. John's team always came in last among the other 23 teams, and its members could never hit performance targets quite so well as their counterparts. At one no-holds-barred session we attended, one woman broke down in tears when she addressed John: "You and Steve (the plant's general manager) are forcing us to be a team, and we don't want to be."

We had seen enough of these kinds of sessions to know that seldom do the members of a group collectively decide that they don't want to be a team, even if they are aware that it takes a long time and effort to develop that synergy. No, there were other issues here that needed to be surfaced.

As both the team leader and an individual, John demonstrated tremendous courage in his willingness to listen to complaints and suggestions in such a public forum as this session presented. Encouraged to speak their minds, team members expressed their anger about John's lack of support and direction and his absence in spirit when the team hit a wall and needed a boost to overcome a problem. John sat quietly, taking notes and listening intently.

After months of open communication and repairing some team damage, positive results emerged. The team, with John on board, decided to meet twice a week to discuss issues and to solve problems that were plaguing their internal customers. Gradually the gloom that hung over the entire team began to lift as their positive energy increased. Still the leader, John had become a respected leader in the eyes of his fellow team members.

Over the next two years, this team grew both emotionally and professionally. Completing their next round of self-observations, they found that they had indeed become a team rather than a collection of individuals wearing the same logos on their shirts. From top management to shop floor employees, everyone saw the difference both in attitude and in performance. As for John, his new leadership style received kudos from people inside and outside the plant, and within one year he was promoted to the corporate office— not bad for a guy who just a year or so earlier had reduced some of his team members to tears. Now those same team members were singing a different song, praising not only John's success but also their own for the progress they had made as a team.

When we helped bring together members for a new team, we stress the importance of the individuals functioning as a cohesive unit from the outset. They must not think of themselves as a committee, with one person representing marketing, another there to protect the interests of the purchasing department, and so on. Instead of someone saying, "Well, I've done my design piece," or "I've given my financial statement," and then sitting back to wait for someone else to produce the deliverable, the entire team must ask, "How can we all do this together?"

To foster the necessary cooperative attitude and to increase productivity, we emphasize the necessity of bringing teams together to work in a central location, a process known as *colocating*. At Disney these locations are called "planning centers," and the company has found that its people are much more efficient and willing to take the initiative when they can discuss a problem or ask questions of someone sitting nearby. Brainstorming sessions have a way of happening spontaneously under colocated conditions.

A couple of years ago, Tom Allen, a professor at MIT, did a study determining the relationship between communication and distance in the workplace. For six months, he examined the communication patterns among 512 employees in seven organizations. He found that at a distance of 30 feet or less, the quality of communication is five times better than it is at a distance of 100 feet. Allen's research also showed that beyond 100 feet, distance is immaterial because communication is simply ineffective—period. In other words, ease of communication is largely dependent on physical location.[12]

Even before we saw this scientific study, we had reached a similar conclusion from our own experience. When questions need to be asked or issues discussed, proximity enables inter- action. It was with the idea of bringing people together to facilitate communication and improve production that Chrysler began in 1990 a five-year plan to redesign its engi- neering facilities at a cost of $1 billion. Bringing together all major engineering functions into one facility, this physical reorganization contributed substantially to the revival of the company.[13]

But a word of warning: We have seen many companies move their people into open work spaces on the mistaken assumption that they have then created a team. When nothing constructive emerges from this arrangement, they disband the so-called team and label it a failure. They have misunderstood the purpose of colocating. The open work space does not, in itself, create a team. It is merely a tool that is used to *reinforce* the team concept. To be successful, a team must also have a mission and goal and be dedicated to fostering the progress of that goal. As on the playing field, the team in a manufacturing plant, an office, or corporate headquarters has to work as a unit, not a collection of individual efforts, no matter what stars you recruit for the key positions. The greatest third baseman, running back, or point guard in the world cannot make a group of people into a "team." That comes only with leadership, com- mitment to a goal that everyone agrees is worth pursuing,

It almost goes without saying that some type of reward sys- tem should be in place to recognize superior performance. However, most managers we encounter feel that a little bit of healthy individual competition is as important, if not more important, than teamwork. They really believe competition is good for the organization and will even boost productivity. Most of us have been encouraged since we were very young to compete with one another in school as well as sports. People rationalize that a competitive spirit is a simple fact of human nature.

Alfie Kohn, author of *No Contest: The Case Against Competition* has spent more than a decade reviewing the effects of competition and cooperation in hundreds of organizations. His conclusion is quite clear: "Superior performance not only does not require competition; it seems to require its absence."[14] David and Roger Johnson of the University of Minnesota report the following results from an educational environment study: 173 studies found that cooperation promotes higher achievement than competition or independent efforts, whereas 13 studies found that competition promotes higher achievement. Another 78 studies found no significant statistical difference.[15]

Red Auerbach, the indefatigable coach of the Boston Celtics, who won 16 NBA championships under his direction, never kept individual statistics on his players. Hubie Brown, the basketball commentator and former coach, remembers the Celtic style that Auerbach helped create: "Red knew how to push the right button on each guy to get him to be subservient to the team...The Celtics understood the maxim, 'There is no I in *Team*.'"[16]

The benefits of a team reward system as opposed to a competitive one are so compelling that even in a competitive society we must take notice. Everyone benefits from feeling appreciated, and team rewards are an excellent way to encourage the hoped-for sense of community and cohesiveness among team members.

In our work with the global team at Whirlpool, we challenged the organization to weight the reward system more heavily toward team performance instead of individual performance. We believe that when teams achieve exceptional results, appropriate bonuses and pay raises should go to the entire team, not just to certain people that the organization judges to be key contributors. Anything else undermines the entire structure of effective teamwork. If everyone is truly working together toward a common goal, then everyone should be rewarded equally.

In the case of Whirlpool, the global team leader was forced to go to bat for the team to ensure equal recognition. He argued that the combined efforts of each and every team member made his group one of the top-rated performers in the entire company. Furthermore, he insisted on equality, and he offered to give up his own personal bonus to get it.

This leader exhibited exceptional integrity and commitment in his battle to secure the proper recognition for his teammates, but it's not always necessary to go to such great lengths to reward team members. In fact, rewards don't have to be in the form of money and prizes. A reward can be something as simple as a pizza party over the lunch hour. In some cases, we've worked with executives who chose to host a barbecue, actually cooking the burgers and hot dogs and serving the team themselves. A personal effort is a particularly effective way of showing appreciation. As Dr. Bill Cross of Mead Johnson says, "I think that [teamwork] is making the workplace more relaxed, and work ought to be fun, if you can use that term. And we are trying to make work fun and it is succeeding to a large extent."[17]

We also encourage teams to develop their own celebrations. When management is comfortable encouraging this—and certainly not all management can do it—team members gain an added sense of empowerment. They can say, "This is really our team, so let's decide together how we want to celebrate." But whether it's a function of management or of the team itself, the important thing is to plan at the beginning for some type of rewards as team members reach and exceed their goals.

CONCRETE RESULTS

Teams have a variety of roles and potential uses. We have set them up to examine customer complaints and determine their root causes. We have structured teams around process reengineering. We have asked outside suppliers to come and join in discussions about partnering possibilities in purchasing, engineering, and manufacturing functions. We have created steering teams whose role is to oversee the whole team process.

Teams can be set up for a specific, one-time goal, of course, but we always suggest that they continue to function on an ongoing basis after they have fulfilled their primary purpose. Even though the group will probably meet for only about an hour a week, the proper harnessing of this collective energy can produce worthwhile results.

At Lensing Wholesale, we helped set up teams that have functioned continually since 1993. The steering team, made up of the owners of the company, sponsors new teams as different needs arise. Some of the teams are issue and process oriented, but most are natural work teams that follow organizational lines and take care of specific work problems.

The adoption of the team system has made a concrete difference at Lensing, in its relations not only with suppliers and customers but also with employees, who now feel empowered to voice their opinions when they believe that a process can be changed for the better.

One of the managers, Donnie Montgomery, started his career at Lensing by working as a handler for one of the company's products, Pella Windows. Recognizing this warehouse worker's potential, his supervisor, Mike O'Donohue, proposed him for the manager's job when the previous manager left. Mike initially had a difficult time persuading the company president, Joe Theby, that Donnie was up to the task. It was, after all, a big jump from handler to manager. But Mike's foresight proved to be absolutely on target.

We met Donnie when the company sent him to us for training as a team leader. It seems that not only had he performed superbly on a day-to-day basis, but working in a team setting had encouraged him to develop an innovative new trucking schedule. It was this initiative that had so impressed Joe.

Illinois Power, another of our clients that adopted a team-based structure, also has witnessed results worth noting. After the utility executives decided to introduce total quality management, we helped to set up some 475 teams that brought more than 80 percent of the workforce into the decision-making process. The ideas that emerged from these teams played a significant part in the changed management effort. The teams submitted more than 2500 suggestions to save money or increase revenue, which, when implemented, produced net savings of more than $18 million per year! Teams also came up with nearly 3000 ideas for improving the work process or customer service.

Teams have taken on very specific functions at the Mead Johnson Nutritional Division of Bristol-Myers Squibb. Initially, 55 teams were organized, of which 7 were process teams, 10 dealt with issues, 32 were natural work groups, 5 were set up as steering teams, and 1 was to be a catchall for any special issues that came up.

At the start, the unit known as the Track Team established its purpose and its goals: "Our mission is to improve the cycle time involved with tracing and expediting, to increase the quality of the response, and to assure our customers that Mead Johnson provides a reliable service."

Tracing and expediting were handled by different departments, so the team began its work by making flow charts of the process used in dealing with customers' orders. The team discovered that the company had received 2267 requests to trace an order in the previous year and that each request had taken more than a half-hour to complete. In the same year, 3117 orders had to be expedited.

The team also surveyed customers to ascertain their expectations and problems and to hear their suggestions or criticisms. This information was then coordinated on a flow chart, which enabled the team to change the functions of various departments.

Participants recounted instances of needless bureaucratic paper shuffling stemming from the fact that the tracing and expediting system was managed by various departments. When a customer called to ask for information about the status of an order, for example, the request went from department to department, requiring that time be spent filling out multiple tracer forms and resulting in the frequent need to request information more than once.

The team remedied the system's shortcomings by allowing the relevant departments to do their own tracing with private carriers, which saved the company thousands of dollars annually.

After investigating true transit times of orders, the team further determined that expediting was unnecessary because regular carriers already offered customers the quickest possible transit time. The team decided that except in the case of a special customer request, normal order-taking procedures would be substituted for formerly expedited shipments. The benefits accruing from this reform added up to about 1140 hours and additional savings.

Deliveries that previously would have gone out on Saturdays by Federal Express were eliminated. The team also suggested that the paperwork on tracer forms be omitted since the information was now stored in a computer. All in all, the team's recommendations saved the company thousands of dollars a year.

A summary at the close of the Track Team's report underscored the advantages of implementing change through teamwork:

> This experience has opened the eyes of some non-believers and has confirmed to others that this process and new environment is possible and will achieve success. With the proper guidance through training and experience, a new culture of team building closely associated with trust within the ranks will soon become the norm instead of the exception.[18]

Trust is at the core of the value system of any organization that expects to equip anyone on its payroll at any level and at any time to solve customer problems. Trust is the interpersonal principle that needs to be in alignment with the personal, managerial, and organizational levels in a progressive culture.

Trust cannot exist without people themselves being trustworthy. They must share the values and possess the skills needed to meet and exceed customer expectations. If you want your organization to be truly customer-driven, you must give your employees control in assisting each and every customer they serve. In most environments, however, only certain individuals are entrusted and empowered to this degree.

As Father Carl of Abbey Press put it,

> We are definitely talking more about the customer here at Abbey Press. Our teams are more focused on how to work better together making the best use of their time to try to get

something done. They also do a good job of taking assignments away from meetings and working independently or in smaller teams to expedite the process of improving the overall business processes. These are all real powerful benefits.

A COLLECTIVE EFFORT OR AN EFFORT AT COLLECTING?

Father Carl's is a positive appraisal to be sure, and one that confirms our belief in the power of teams. Yet we would be remiss if we did not recognize that some companies have had mixed results with teams. The synergy just isn't developed, or there may be a lack of energy and inspiration. In fact, some situations simply aren't suited to the team concept at all. These drawbacks raise the danger that cynicism will creep in and overshadow the importance and potential value of teams.

Thus, it's important to recognize that when teams work well, they are spectacularly successful in solving problems and delivering results quickly and cost-effectively. At their best—and we have seen many that rate that superlative description—teams are about harnessing the collective talents of a diverse group of employees. The sum is far greater than the parts, and that adds up to an important tool for companies that want to wind up on the winning side.

A company that has recognized the power of collective effort is primed for the next phase of the Believe principle: Go outside the corporate family to draw on the talents of suppliers and partners. In Chapter 6, we'll look at what secure, long-term external alliances can mean for your organization.

Questions to Ask
- Is the "not invented here" excuse used to block the development of teams?
- Does the physical layout of offices and other work areas prohibit the easy sharing of ideas and the formation of teams?
- Do your teams receive the recognition and rewards they deserve?

- Do some employees have an undue sense of owning a product, an idea, or a process? Do you encourage cooperation rather than competition among employees?

- Is team formation part of any job description or training program? Do you have both natural work teams and cross-functional teams in place?

- Does the company provide the necessary tools, e.g., a local area network (LAN), for encouraging people to share their knowledge and ideas?

- Do your leaders demonstrate buy-in to a team culture?

- Have your teams written mission statements or set goals (in writing) that are aligned with those of the organization as a whole?

- Are your teams "colocated" for ease of communication and project management?

- Do you encourage teams to enlist the help of qualified facilitators when necessary?

Actions to Take
- Use multifunctional teams for all product-development or process-reengineering activities.

- Be aware of shared resources; you need total commitment that is colocated.

- Develop team rewards.

- Hire team-creation specialists.

- Study other companies with successful teams.

- Increase organizationwide information sharing.

- Hire and promote coworkers who demonstrate a cooperative style.

- Examine the physical layout of the workplace and colocate teams in a systematic fashion to make the best use of the space.

- Provide well-trained facilitators upon whom team members can call as needed.

- Celebrate and reward team accomplishments.

- Periodically refocus and rebuild teams in a retreat setting.

WORKING AS A TEAM

One of the problems that Jerry McColgin had faced in his previous team experience was the fact that the members were dispersed throughout company facilities. This time, he insisted, the entire team had to work within four walls. The company agreed and found four abandoned product-display rooms for the team's use.

The company made a further commitment by underwriting the physical construction of the space. Walls were torn down, new lighting and new carpeting installed, and desks moved. An active noise system (ANS) was also introduced into the large open space. An ANS adds "pink noise," a combination of frequencies that match the human voice to the environment. Noise was an issue. Some of the members were used to working in a private office, and the fact that the place was a modern-day Tower of Babel made it hard to tune out foreign voices. A year later, when the system was turned off as an experiment, everyone begged for it to be turned on again.

Everything was brand new for the team, which, as Jerry noted, "Right from the outset sent a signal that this was a unique project, something different, something that had never been done. Nobody had ever had us all sit together like this."

Colocating also sent a valuable message to the team itself. Clearly, the company was backing the project completely, which was a welcome signal that they had faith the team could get the job done.

To facilitate the work, the overall team was divided into subteams. These, however, remained cross functional, so that people still intermingled. "I would walk through the room," Jerry remembers, "and I'd see a manufacturing engineer and a design engineer pouring over blueprints, each giving their input. Instead of waiting for a Monday morning meeting, the discussion was taking place there and then, when it was needed. One of the things the team prided itself on was the absolute lack of bureaucracy."

No pieces of paper had to be pushed through the system to be initialed by a management hierarchy. As a matter of fact, as Jerry had promised at the outset, there was no hierarchy.

SHARE THE SPOTLIGHT

When we team up, it creates a winning combination.

KEN POTROCK

Vice President, Alliance Marketing,
Walt Disney World Resort

In the world arena, the United States has watched its competitive advantage slip away over the past half-century or so. Where once the United States had a per capita gross national product 4 times that of Germany and 15 times that of Japan, the three are now, in broad terms, relatively equal contenders.

How did this happen? Quite simply, Japan and Germany used partnerships to propel themselves out of their weakened post-World War II states of economic disarray to become strong competitors in one industry after another. What's more, as the end of the 20th century approaches, an even bigger competitive threat is posed by the European Community, and what is this largest of world economic markets if not the product of true partnership?

If American companies are to rise to the competitive challenges that lie ahead, they too, must reap the benefits of partnering. Admittedly, successful partnering does not come easily to most of us. As Broadway composer Charles Strouse's lyrics proclaim, applause is what "we're living for," and top billing makes that applause ever so sweet. But when it comes to getting things accomplished in the business world, the savvy competitor will recognize the value of drawing on the expertise and resources of others. In fact, the wise man or woman already knows that it is a fortuitous combination of talents that most often produces the applause-winning achievement. The key is turning that knowledge into practical action.

The solution lies in examining the methods of companies that are topflight competitors at home and abroad. The Walt Disney Company is a rich sourcebook of partnering expertise that is ours for the taking.

PARTNERSHIPS EXPAND THE POSSIBILITIES

Walt Disney certainly had his share of individual success, becoming a cultural icon around the world because of his many achievements. But even though he was blessed with creative genius, surefire entertainment instincts, and an astute commercial sense, Walt recognized early on that strong alliances were necessary to achieve what one could not achieve alone.

Were it not for his first partnership with his brother Roy, for example, Walt Disney might have remained an obscure animator and cartoonist. When the Disney Brothers Studio opened in 1923, Roy invested his entire savings of $200 in the venture, and it was Roy who took over the finances—such as they were—in those early days. This family partnership had its rocky moments, to be sure—one breach lasted years. But in the final analysis, the two brothers accomplished much more in partnership than either could have done alone. Without Roy's assistance, Mickey, Donald, Pluto, and the host of other beloved Disney characters might well have remained nothing more than figments of Walt's imagination.

Walt knew, too, that not only must an alliance work for both partners, but each partner must work at forming and maintaining a successful affiliation. A partnership is, after all, an investment in the future, and just like any other investment, it must be carefully considered and skillfully managed to produce the optimum return. What's more, you must know who your partner is and be sure she shares your values.

The latter lesson is one that Walt learned all too painfully in one of his first deals made outside the family orbit, a disastrous partnership with the distributor of his *Oswald the Rabbit* cartoons. Disney originally signed a contract with a New York distributor, Margaret Winkler. Trouble began when she married and her husband, Charles Mintz, took over her business. In a 1926 distribution deal involving Universal Pictures, Mintz persuaded the Disney brothers—whom he always referred to as "the bumpkins"—to create a new cartoon to compete with the very popular *Felix the Cat*. The result was the imaginative and successful *Oswald* series.

Mintz, however, was determined to acquire the Disney studio. When the distribution contract expired, he cut the studio's payments by nearly a third and threatened to take over the operation. After all, according to the contract, he owned *Oswald*. Walt was devastated, but he had no choice other than to comply with the contract.

That contract, however, was limited solely to *Oswald*, and Walt was free to create new characters. In the end, the *Oswald* fiasco proved to be a serendipitous turn of events, because the failed partnership led to the birth of Mickey Mouse. But Walt never forgot that partnering with like-minded people is critical to the success of the relationship. One need only look at the list of highly touted mergers gone awry to understand the value of the lesson Walt learned so early in his career. Philosophical and cultural differences are frequently cited as the reason these unions fail.

PARTNERSHIPS TAKE MANY FORMS

Business partnerships are entered into for a variety of reasons, of course. Some are formed to carry out a specific project, whereas others are joined on a long-term basis, like law partnerships.

One of Walt Disney's first remunerative partnerships was with a small New York stationery firm. He signed a contract giving the firm the rights to sell school children's writing pads with a portrait of Mickey Mouse printed on them. The firm paid a mere $300 for the rights, but it was 1929 and Disney was broke and eager for every nickel he could get.

"As usual, Roy and I needed the money," he said later.

Although on its face the deal was a small one, it opened Disney's eyes to the possibilities of making money through ancillary uses of his creative product. He never overlooked an opportunity to do so from then on, and licensing arrangements became central to his management philosophy. A couple of years later, he licensed the sale of Mickey Mouse watches, which initially sold at the rate of about one million per year. Other similar agreements brought in 10 percent of the company's income over a decade-long period. All the while, Walt kept a sharp eye out for any violations of his copyright, just as the Disney Company does today.

But even Walt could not have dreamt of the multimillion-dollar cornucopia of Disney products that has evolved from that first Mickey Mouse school tablet. The company licenses its cartoon characters to manufacturers, and products bearing the names and pictures of those characters are then sold by retailers around the world. There are company-owned and operated stores, as well as a Disney Web site that markets movies, books, art, clothing, jewelry, collectibles, and a host of other products all bearing the likeness of various familiar Disney figures and all produced under license from the Walt Disney Company.

Most of Disney's numerous partnerships were formed for purely business reasons, but one of his most unlikely affiliations stemmed from a creative communion that developed quite by chance. One evening Walt was eating alone in a fashionable Hollywood restaurant when he spotted the famous conductor of the Philadelphia Orchestra, Leopold Stokowski, also dining alone. He invited Stokowski to join him. Stokowski was a giant in the world of classical music, and with his mane of white hair and sweeping gestures, he looked every inch the *maestro,* whether leading an orchestra or chatting with a friend over dinner.

Discussing future plans, Disney mentioned that he was about to start work on a new Mickey Mouse cartoon, *The Sorcerer's Apprentice.* Stokowski expressed an interest in conducting the score and even offered to waive his fee. Over the dinner table, the two men then discussed the possibility of making an animated feature set to the music of great composers. Out of this conversation grew the 1940 movie *Fantasia*. Disney and Stokowski were equally charmed by the concept.

In the film, Stokowski conducted everything from Beethoven to the avant-garde music of Igor Stravinsky, while animated figures interpreted the compositions through dance. Visual interpretation of orchestral music was a new concept, and *Fantasia* won raves from the critics. Bosley Crowther of *The New York Times* called it "simply terrific, as terrific as anything that has ever happened on the screen," while another critic described it as "a new artistic experience of great beauty." Because it was so unlike any other Disney movie, however, the public rejected it. Today though, the film is highly regarded, especially among film historians.

The partnership with Stokowski served Disney well in a creative and artistic sense, and represented a great step forward in the fusion of animation, color, and sound. And even though the film was, at the time, a financial failure, Walt viewed few things as absolute failures. He knew that even unsuccessful ventures provide valuable lessons, and such hard-won knowledge can be put to use elsewhere.

Taking its cue from Walt, the Disney Company does not consign failed projects to the trash heap. Rather, it considers them to be assets of the company that may be tried again later or perhaps utilized in a different capacity. What the company learned from the poor audience reception of the original *Fantasia* in 1940 will no doubt be put to use in the new version now in the works, *Fantasia 2000*.

PARTNERSHIPS CAN SECURE PROSPERITY

Partnerships were obviously an integral part of Walt Disney's business strategy, often serving as lifelines in times of financial distress. In the 1930s alone, a string of partnerships—ranging from an exclusive arrangement with Technicolor and licensing contracts that put Mickey and Minnie's faces on toys and clothes to deals for a syndicated newspaper comic strip and a deal for the publication of the *Mickey Mouse Book*—pulled the company back from the edge of bankruptcy. At this particular time in Walt's career, the cash flow from cartoons was little more than a trickle (he often had to wait months to be paid by his distributors), and the partnerships were crucial to survival.

During the building of Disneyland in the 1950s, Walt again found himself short of cash. Even though ABC invested $500,000 and guaranteed a bank loan of $4.5 million, the price tag for finishing the park came to some $17 million. Walt cashed in his life insurance policy and then began to search for ways to close the financing gap. The novel solution he came up with was corporate sponsorships, which, in effect, are another form of partnership. Disney signed agreements with the Coca-Cola Company and with the Eastman Kodak Company, giving them exclusive concessions at Disneyland. He also signed up small, unknown partners, even allowing a corset maker and a real estate agent to set up shop in the park.

In building Disney World, the company took the same tack, entering agreements that gave the likes of Exxon, AT&T, and General Motors pavilion space at EPCOT. EPCOT is, in fact, a testimony to partnership. And when Michael Eisner and Frank Wells took over the leadership of the Disney Company in 1984, 18 years after Walt's death and 13 years after the opening of Disney World, these original partnerships were still contributing thousands annually to the Disney coffers.

Although the Disney partnerships have certainly helped it fend off disaster at times, the company has never looked at partnerships simply as stopgap measures forced on it by market conditions. Quite the opposite, partnerships are viewed as long-term investments in the company's future prosperity. Corporate sponsorships and the income they generate support this. But the company continues to exemplify, just as Walt did, the principle that alliances must work for both partners if they are to endure. Company executives must thus be willing to commit themselves to cooperating fully, trusting implicitly, and communicating effectively with partners. Even though the relationship may be a business deal, personal contact will help to cement it.

Indicative of how much the company values the personal touch is the three-day get-together Eisner planned prior to the Disney-Capital Cities/ABC merger in 1996. The CEO invited 200 people—executives and their spouses—from ABC television and the Disney Company to the Disney Institute in Florida so that the two companies could build a more personal relationship.

Eisner is well aware that a partnership is bound to fail if left to its own devices. It takes nurturing, hand-holding, head-cracking, and once in a while, even arm-twisting. Partnerships can be both delicate and resilient, but they always demand constant vigilance.

RESTRUCTURING TOTAL QUALITY THROUGH PARTNERING

Business alliances, as we said, are formed for any number of reasons. There is partnering between customer and supplier and between managers and co-workers. There is also partnering between manufacturing and service companies; between business, community, and educational institutions; and between government and industry. In our consulting business, we have encouraged a multitude of organizations to consider "restructuring total quality through partnerships." By this we mean a coming together of suppliers, manufacturers, and service providers in much the same way that Japanese companies work together to support and strengthen one another's positions. We envision quality performance through teamwork.

CERTIFICATION VS. PARTNERSHIPS

In the 1980s, customer/supplier partnerships were defined by a process of vendor certification. The process required the vendor to adopt a new culture that entailed meeting a wide range of quality and product standards. In effect, the vendor's performance was constantly tested against a set of standards designed to conform to the needs of the customer.

Moreover, one vendor was leveraged against another because organizations insisted on having two or three sources for the same item. Often a vendor was required to reduce prices to remain competitive, regardless of the impact on the vendor's organization. The rationale for the price cuts lay in the expectation that the vendor should constantly be improving processes and sharing the resultant savings with the customer.

While certification streamlined the buying process, strategic direction was developed without vendor input. Thus, little was done to improve the competitive position of either the customer or the supplier.

In contrast, true partnerships envision working with vendors to develop compatible cultures. If sole-source relationships are developed, win-win performance measures can be devised that take into consideration the needs of both parties. In addition, sole-source relationships encourage process integration and the cross-company sharing of results. Vendors can more readily be included in strategic planning. The end result is an efficient and productive alliance for both suppliers and customers. Indeed, the term *partnership* presupposes the willingness not only to share the spotlight but also to work out in a straightforward fashion what is best for both parties. Sometimes these arrangements aren't bound by legal contracts and actually bear more of a resemblance to the kind of teamwork we discussed in the preceding chapter.

One of our clients, for example, established an innovative and productive relationship with the company that supplies its packaging. Constant problems and the words "this isn't working" marked the association between the two companies before they decided to set up an informal partnership. Now, teams comprising staff members from each company consult with one another about a variety of issues: the design of the packaging so that it meets precise specifications; the costs involved; the materials to be used, and so forth. Engineers, purchasing agents, and managers from each company now meet regularly to discuss their respective needs. The two companies work so closely together that some of the packaging-supply people have desks at our client's offices, and a new computer network keeps everyone informed of progress on issues of mutual interest.

To confirm that it was on the right track with this informal arrangement, our client compared the costs of using traditional purchasing methods against the costs of its new method. The new procedure won hands down, and it is producing substantial cost savings. Equally gratifying, this collaboration has produced a welcome reduction in material needs, a critical factor at a time when forest shrinkage is reducing the supply of wood pulp.

A close alliance is also producing big rewards for Wal-Mart and Bristol-Myers Squibb, which supplies the discount retailer with its products on a quick-delivery basis. As the products are sold, Wal-Mart's purchasing department informs the sales department at Bristol-Myers and replacement products are shipped out within 24 hours. The partnership has worked so well that Wal-Mart chose to honor Bristol-Myers as a Supplier of the Month, not because of size, for many of Wal-Mart's thousands of suppliers dwarf Bristol-Myers in terms of volume, but because of reliability.

The Disney Company has long understood the importance of respecting its suppliers and maintaining strong alliances with them. Michael Vance, former head of Disney University, tells the story of when he and Roy Disney visited the construction site during the building of Disney World. As the two men entered the site, the first thing they saw was a large sign announcing, ALL CONTRACTORS *IMMEDIATELY* REPORT TO CONSTRUCTION SHACK 47 UPON ENTERING THE PREMISES.

Reading that clear and curt order, Roy turned to Mike and asked, "What does that convey to you?"

Without hesitation, Vance responded, "It says that we don't trust our suppliers to be on the property."

"Right," Disney replied. "And who's responsible for communicating the Disney culture and values to all employees on the property?"

As it happens, that is one of the goals of the Disney University, so Vance put together a team that designed and built a new reception center. Now contractors and construction workers at Disney World are treated like the valued partners they are. The reception center offers them coffee and Cokes, telephones, and meeting rooms, all in a pleasant and welcoming atmosphere.

As Roy Disney explained to Vance, not only were company values at stake but also the wider reputation of the company. "We need to be partners with our contractors for the park to open on time, but even more importantly, they have to be proud to be a part of this, so they will call friends and family all over the country and tell them to come down to see what they've done."

LESSONS RELEARNED

Do any of us *always* follow the rules, even though those rules may stem from our own stated convictions? Probably not.

EuroDisney is a case in point for Disney. Even though partnerships have always been central to Disney's business strategy, the company deviated from standard practice when it came to building the French park. At both of its domestic sites, for example, Disney retained a percentage of the hotel rooms (14 percent at Disney World) and also entered into partnerships with other hotels, such as the Sheraton chain. But management avoided partnership arrangements with any French hotels, which meant that the rooms were not furnished to French tastes. For example, the French expect fireplaces in their vacation villas and Disney had neglected this detail. Today, Disney has corrected this problem by retrofitting each room with a fireplace.

One of the biggest mistakes, though, was in naming the park. The French are enormously proud of their country and their culture, and they greatly resented the lack of a French identity in the EuroDisney name. In this instance, the entire population of France was, in effect, Disney's partner, and in forgetting the lesson Walt took away from the Oswald calamity, that is, to know and understand your partner's culture and values, the company made a serious error.

Fortunately, Disney took steps to rectify the problems before the venture failed completely. Today, the park is known as Disneyland Paris, and refinancing has established partnerships within the business community. Not surprisingly, the park is beginning to show real signs of a successful turnaround.

At home, too, the company has suffered the consequences of reneging on the implicit partnership it maintains with employees. When problems arose with the Disney Golf Resort Hotel, for example, management went through the motions of welcoming frontline input, then promptly rejected it.

To determine why the Golf Resort's occupancy rate hovered in the low 90 percent range while every other Disney World hotel was actually over 100 percent by having guests on a waiting list, management called its reservations staff together. "The problem," the staff said, "is in the name. Most reservations are made by wives. When they see the word *golf*, warning signals go up. They don't want their husbands to spend vacation days on the golf course instead of joining in the family fun at the park. So they request reservations at one of the other hotels."

Management's reaction was incredulous: "You guys don't know what you're talking about."

Dismissing the opinion of the very people who dealt with would-be guests on a daily basis, the company hired a marketing firm, which, lo and behold, came up with exactly the same answer. Red-faced and apologetic, management went back to the reservations staff to get suggestions for a new name. The name The Disney Inn was eventually selected as a suitably neutral alternative to The Golf Resort.

As the above examples indicate, Disney has occasionally made the mistake of ignoring its standards for working in partnership. And every time, management has had to backtrack when the mistake was recognized and reembrace its time-tested principles. No matter how big or how successful a company becomes, partnership, with other companies, employees, suppliers, customers, or the community, is a valuable asset that needs to be cultivated.

Partnerships are being cultivated and used in creative ways by a diverse range of organizations. One of the most novel partnerships we ever participated in occurred some years back when we were working with the School of Nursing at the University of Southern Indiana. A dispute arose over the amount of continuing education that was available to the nursing faculty. The nurses wanted more, but the administration said there was simply no money for such a program.

Having already established a team at the school during a strategic planning retreat, we worked with team members to devise a simple but ingenious solution to the dispute. The school approached a local hospital and offered to staff a unit for one shift a week, using student nurses from the school. The fee to the hospital was less than the hospital's usual staffing cost for the hours involved, the students got credit for practical experience, and the school used the money from the hospital to fund courses in continuing education for the faculty. It was a deal in which everyone came out a winner.

Another result of good partnerships is that they often lead to welcome but perhaps unexpected outcomes. At Asea Brown Boveri of Canada, for example, a partnership with customers helped turn around one of the electrical engineering concern's faltering regional operations. A new manager, who was sent in by headquarters to boost revenues, eschewed the traditional approaches of making changes in product and processes, and of downsizing. Instead, he asked staff members to find out the needs and problems of the businesses in their marketing area. He also established partnerships with local business people to explore potential areas of improvement. In only one year, the new manager's unorthodox reliance on a partnering approach with customers began to pay off as the operation returned to profitability.

In Evansville, Indiana, a communitywide quality initiative established by the Metropolitan Chamber of Commerce with our assistance, is helping to align the objectives of business and government. The stated mission of the program is "to promote, educate, facilitate, and recognize the use of continuous improvement...among the regional community's organizations and enterprises, resulting in economic growth and improved quality of life."

Local businesses, local and regional government offices, and educational institutions are working as partners to achieve this ambitious goal. Teams made up of company, government, and educational representatives have been established to ensure that Evansville will be able to provide the caliber of worker needed in the rapidly changing workplace. Yearly conferences bring all the participants together to assess progress toward the goals and to facilitate communications.

Yet another example of partnering between industry and government involves Kentucky Technology Service (KTS), Inc., of Louisville. KTS is a nonprofit institution dedicated to facilitating effective communication between the various regional agencies that have been set up to help small manufacturers solve engineering and production problems. As part of its program, KTS enlists various educational institutions, from major universities to four-year and community colleges, to provide training to its clients.

Recognizing that its various efforts were badly disjointed, KTS approached us for assistance in reducing duplication among the regional agencies and in establishing an educational consortium. We also encouraged KTS to make the government/educational partnership function more effectively by zeroing in on the specific needs of manufacturers in diverse areas of the state.

Now KTS is a shining example of how wide-ranging partnerships between industry and government, and between educational institutions and the communities they serve, are forming a complex web of support that is strengthening the position of each partner.

It almost goes without saying that when people from varying backgrounds and endeavors are involved, some glitches are bound to develop along the way. But if all participants are prepared at the outset for this eventuality, with a little give-and-take, most such difficulties can be smoothed out. The key to effective working alliances is sustained communication between all the participants and a genuine understanding of the purpose of the association. The overriding value of the partnership must not be tarnished by minor problems.

With that in mind, we urge you to identify your key suppliers and partners and then make an honest effort to spend time with them so that you can begin to understand each other's needs. Organize dream-type retreats where you can identify customer problems and customer dreams. Build long-term relationships in which you share the spotlight with "costars."

Our work with numerous companies large and small has made abundantly clear the power that is generated when two or more organizations direct their creative energies to solving shared problems. Mastering the art of partnering can give your organization the confidence to wholeheartedly embrace the third concept in the Disney quartet: Dare!

In the next chapter, we will look at what it means to take calculated risks and how an organization can thrive on the opportunities that arise when one is willing to accept a challenge.

Questions to Ask
- Do you trust the judgment of your employees and treat them as partners?
- Does your organization have true alliances with suppliers?
- Do you routinely meet with your suppliers to involve them in strategic planning?
- Do you believe that the best ideas often come from those outside your own organization?

Actions to Take
- Gain feedback from employees on a regular basis by asking the following questions: (1) How are we doing as a company in developing partnerships with employees? (2) Do we invite your input and creativity on problems and solutions on organizational issues? (3) How are we doing as a company in developing partnerships with our suppliers?
- Invite employees to investigate organizational issues by identifying barriers to success and encourage them to develop solutions.

- Meet with suppliers two days or more per quarter to discuss ways to solve customer problems and fulfill customer dreams.

SUPPLIERS AS PARTNERS

Of course, when a radical new design for a product is initiated, the costs are high. Changes have to be made in basic drawings and design. Then bids are put out to suppliers, who must, in turn, redesign their products. "This is going to cost you an extra $5000 because we have to retool," is often the suppliers' answer.

The Global No-Frost team tried a different and innovative approach. As the work moved forward, the team became involved with the company's capital equipment suppliers, who were supplying the equipment for the plant in India. The structure was to be built on an empty site in the middle of a wasteland on the outskirts of Pune, near Bombay. There were some 10 equipment suppliers, and the company was spending, at the very least, $5000 with each one.

The team set up an unprecedented two-day meeting with all the suppliers. The meeting opened with Jerry standing up and informing his audience that first of all, everyone would have to sign a confidentiality agreement to protect the company. Then, he continued, "Traditionally, you're told exactly what is wanted, but this time it will be different. I want you to understand how your contribution fits into the overall project." He proceeded to explain the whole schedule and where each supplier fitted in. "I pointed out as well that our success was entirely dependent on them."

The response was amazing. They were thrilled to be included and to understand their role in the process. Usually, suppliers' contact with the company is limited to one manufacturing engineer. Now they were dealing with 35 people as a team. To keep them abreast of developments, they were sent a monthly update, which not only included an account of the team's progress but also mentioned suppliers who were on time and even more to the point, suppliers who had fallen behind schedule.

A true measure of the team's partnership with suppliers came on the question of one part's specifications. When this particular part is manufactured in North America, a thickness of 3.8 millimeters is required. The suppliers suggested that the part could be produced with a thickness of 2.9 millimeters and function just as well and at considerable savings. Without their early involvement and attention to detail, the planned refrigerator would probably have ended up at the required specification, but too large and too expensive.

When it came to inaugurating the new plant, some of the suppliers came to the dedication—at their own cost. That's how involved they felt in our project.

DARE TO DARE

I really do feel—about business and life—that everybody has to make mistakes. And everybody should be encouraged to feel that if they make mistakes, it's okay.

MICHAEL EISNER

Premier players can be found in all corners of the business world, and one thing they have in common is a willingness to take bold risks. They clearly understand that grasping at a dream requires one to reach beyond the sure thing. Even more, they seem to relish the opportunity. Walt Disney was just such a player.

In fact, if literally there were a cornerstone upon which the Walt Disney Company rested, it would have to be inscribed with one short word: Dare. Throughout the 43 years that Walt ran the company, he dared to meet challenges, he dared to take risks, and ultimately, he dared to excel.

From the time that he decided to produce his first cartoon, Disney pushed the limits of ordinary achievement. He pioneered the use of sound in animated cartoons with *Steamboat Willie*. He signed his contract with Technicolor before the revolutionary process had even been accepted by the industry as a whole and astutely insisted on a two-year exclusive for his cartoons. He originated feature-length cartoons with *Snow White* and defied the odds at a time when no one thought anyone would ever sit through a 90-minute cartoon.

Even Walt's decision to build Disneyland represented a new and risky concept in entertainment. Up to that time, amusement parks had something of an unsavory connotation, an association with the tawdriness of pre-1950s carnivals. It took the vision of Walt Disney to imagine a place that would incorporate historical reconstructions, displays, and rides, and it took the daring of Walt Disney to build it into a world-famous tourist attraction.

The Disney experience illustrates how a company willing to take calculated risks can advance the level of development of a product or service and in the process reap huge rewards. But not all corporate executives and managers fall into this enviable category. Too many opt for the safest route because they fear failure or loss. They allow themselves to get bogged down in corporate bureaucracy, which can keep the management process from flowing as it should.

But such behavior is not written in stone. Companies can change the buttoned-down, risk-avoidance atmosphere that dictates status quo first, innovation later—if at all. We have helped numerous leaders learn to prioritize their objectives and to take a holistic view of their companies, thereby putting risk taking into the proper perspective. In this chapter, we will look at how leaders who dare can take calculated risks and lift their organizations to previously unimagined levels of achievement.

SOLID FUNDAMENTALS SUPPORT RISK TAKING

Psychologists might describe Disney as a born risk taker, someone whose fear of failure was outweighed by the need to tackle new challenges. His more cautious brother, Roy, often referred to him as "crazy" or "wacky." But then Roy was in charge of the family cash box, which in the early days his brother depleted with alarming frequency, leaving it to Roy to persuade bankers to agree to new loans or extend old ones.

The key point is that Walt, although politically and personally conservative by nature, accepted no conventional boundaries when it came to his work. He was sure of his values and beliefs, sure of his own talent and that of his cast members, sure of his instincts, and sure that if given the proper chance, this outstanding combination would eventually prevail.

That is not to say that he jumped at every idea that came his way, but he certainly didn't hesitate to take a chance if a concept met his artistic and financial criteria. First and foremost, of course, any potential project had to pass Walt's trademark "family entertainment" test. But if he felt that a project fit with his vision, he would leap, often ahead of the pack.

Another business giant who is not afraid to take a chance to realize his dreams is Lee Iacocca. His name is so inextricably linked to the Chrysler Corporation that asking whether a particular car is a Chrysler or an Iacocca is not really all that far-fetched—particularly if the car in question happens to be a Dodge or Plymouth minivan purchased in the 1980s. Iacocca hatched the idea for the minivan while he was president of the Ford Motor Company. In fact, as early as 1974, Iacocca drove a minivan prototype put together by one of Ford's product engineers, Harold Sperlich, and two Ford designers.

Iacocca loved the car's roominess, but to work properly, it needed a front-wheel-drive power train, the components for which would have to be designed from scratch, an expensive undertaking. Henry Ford II, Ford's ultraconservative chairman and CEO, balked at taking on the risk and the expense. Henry was still haunted by the memory of Ford's Edsel fiasco some 20 years earlier.

When Iacocca left Ford in 1978, he got permission from William Clay Ford, Henry's younger brother, to take with him the consumer research he had gathered on the minivan. "I didn't know I was going to Chrysler then," Iacocca told *Fortune* magazine in a 1994 interview, "but I had a hankering to do this car because the research was so overpowering."[19]

Harold Sperlich had departed for Chrysler a few years before, so when Iacocca also ended up there, the stage was set for the birth of one of the most profitable consumer products ever built. But first, Iacocca had to find the money to proceed with the minivan project, a daunting prospect at a company that in most quarters had been written off as dead in the water by the time Iacocca took over. The new CEO diverted the money from another project and the rest, as they say, is history.

Like Disney before him, Lee Iacocca dared to follow his instincts while staring potential disaster in the face. Later, with minivan sales surging and a debate raging over whether to commit several hundred million dollars to expand production capacity, Iacocca stood his ground against the opposition of all of his top executives who feared that the minivan might prove to be just a fad. He was sure he had tapped into a huge unanswered market. "Everyone fought me," Iacocca told *Fortune*, "but that's what makes horse races."

Well, not quite. Iacocca had the backing of the solid market research he had done early on, not to mention the strength of his convictions. He wasn't gambling on the unknown; he was taking a calculated risk based on sound numbers and sound instincts.

Both Ford and General Motors had built prototypes of a minivan too, but neither company had the courage to risk investing enough money to bring the vehicle to market. Because of this hesitancy, they lost out to Chrysler.

AVOIDING THE SHORT-TERM MENTALITY

Admittedly, being able to determine whether taking an action or not taking it will put employees and/or customers in jeopardy is not always easy. What's more, some managers are so determined to protect their own turf that they prefer the status quo to any proposition that might threaten their position, no matter how reasonable. This is akin to the "short-term mentality" that we discussed in Chapter 3, and it is the kiss of death for innovation and risk taking. Many great companies have slipped into decline because of this mindset, which combines an inability to take on challenges with a dangerous self-satisfaction with past achievements.

Walt Disney, of course, exhibited the exact opposite of that mindset. When it came to technological advances, for example, he knew that no one could cling to past achievements and survive, so he always had his antennae out for new technology. When the movie industry stubbornly refused to sell or lease any of its products to the television networks in the 1940s and early 1950s, thinking it could stop the juggernaut, Walt took a different view. He saw television's potential market value, and he embraced the opportunities the new medium offered, realizing that it presented yet another outlet for his product.

Although Disney was clever enough to recognize the potential television held, he still spurned the networks' initial approach. As always, Walt was determined to control the environment in which his work was released, and he feared that the black-and-white screen would not do justice to his color cartoons and films.

When he did make a television deal in 1953, he made it with the fledgling American Broadcasting Company, in part because that network agreed to help finance Disneyland. In return, ABC received access to Disney's backlog of films and cartoons. Thus, just as movie audiences were declining markedly in the 1950s, lured away by the flickering screens right in their own living rooms, Disney was cementing an alliance that would plant his product firmly in the new medium. Today, Disney not only has a string of TV successes to its credit, including its own cable channel, it also owns ABC outright.

In our work with the Mead Johnson Nutritional Division of Bristol-Myers Squibb, we encountered a leader who had to make the courageous decision to focus on the long term in the face of very difficult near-term problems.

When we began our talks with this leader, Dr. Bill Cross, who happened to be the division's vice president for quality, his reception to our proposals for change was distinctly lukewarm. Dr. Cross told us later that his first reaction was, "Why do we need to change?" He knew that his division already had a culture of quality and never let bad products go out the door. Then he realized that more than quality was at stake. Dr. Cross began to get excited about implementing a culture where team members could enjoy working together toward common goals and objectives.

As we were laying out plans for the implementation of the change effort and the initial Dream Retreats, Dr. Cross phoned to say that the division was going to have its first-ever layoff in only a few months. "Should the implementation be postponed?" he asked. We couldn't answer his question, of course, because ultimately, the decision was his to make. But in the end, he proceeded as planned. "Okay," he said, "I'm going to plunge ahead because I feel so sure about its worth to us."

Thus, when the layoffs came, the shock that everyone understandably felt was mitigated by the fact that a plan was in place to change the culture to one in which people could enjoy and take pride in their ability to meet customer needs and problems.

After the initial teams were well on their way to success, the vice president took the initiative to enlist the entire division in the change process. Now, the new cultural orientation has spread throughout the unit. It was this leader's belief in the change effort and his recognition that the long-term future of the division was at stake that made the success possible.

Another leader at a *Fortune* 500 manufacturing company with which we work also exemplifies the kind of long-term perspective that Walt Disney showed. Traditionally, manufacturing a new product at this company required the installation of an assembly line costing between $80 million and $100 million. If the product failed, a large investment was lost. Obviously, finding an alternative way of doing things was in the company's best interests.

Deciding to experiment with the possibility of running multiple products on the same assembly line, our client turned to an engineering manager with eight years of service with the company and known as someone willing to experiment to try out new ideas—in short, someone ready to take risks. When the company approached him, however, he was in the enviable position of being head of the division that manufactured the most profitable product in its line.

Although managing this pioneering project carried the possibility of enormous benefits, success was by no means guaranteed. How many leaders would be willing to give up a sure thing to take on a risky, albeit potentially consequential task? Yet rather than fearing failure, this individual was excited about the ultimate goal of limiting capital risk, and he welcomed the chance to take on a new challenge. He was enticed to accept the company's offer by the chance to spearhead something new. "That's how you learn and how the best products are developed," he said.

THE MANY FORMS OF RISK

It is usually taken for granted that risks in the business world are financial, but in our experience, risks come in various forms. A risk might involve change in a leader's personal behavior, management style, or willingness to place more trust in co-workers or lower-level employees. Generally, a number of risks must be taken if a company is to reach its peak performance.

One of our clients was unable to risk making needed behavioral change until he was forced into it by circumstance. He was an executive and part owner of a family company. Within the company, he was perceived as an autocrat. Workers complained about his high-handed behavior and his abrupt way of giving orders. The complaints finally reached the company's CEO after it became clear that the executive in question had completely lost the trust of his workers. The output of his department was suffering, and it was losing money.

During discussions with this executive, we pointed out that discontent with his management style was undermining employee morale, and even worse, affecting his efficiency. He had a tough time accepting our assessment at first, but in the end, he acquiesced. We encouraged him to take what for him was an enormous risk: He empowered his staff by giving them information on business goals and performance and by asking them to participate in problem solving.

After three years of coaching, this executive was finally able to relax control and stop micromanaging everything in his department. He eventually became so comfortable with trusting his employees that he could even skip meetings, thus giving them more say. Because he was able to take a difficult personal risk, he reversed his department's decline.

Over the years, we have discovered that the risk of changing often holds a company or an individual back until the time comes when it is forced to make a choice. Threatened by competition or saddled with a product that has ceased to satisfy contemporary needs, many of our clients have come to us and asked, "What shall we do?"

A few times we've encountered companies that talked a good line when it came to making changes only to discover that all management really wanted, in effect, was to throw up a smoke screen. They planned to go through the motions of change by attending meetings with us, but they had no intention of even attempting to implement the suggested actions.

In some ways, however, such behavior is not all that surprising, because it takes courage to accept the fact that you must change. Some companies are never able to do it, and ultimately, they slip quietly under the waves. But others, such as British Petroleum, manage to summon the resolve to do what must be done. As previously discussed in Chapter 2, management admitted that its resources were fast being depleted and that a complete structural overhaul was needed. Circumstances may have forced management's hand, but it still took courage to risk making the fundamental change required to survive.

SHAKE UP YOUR HIRING POLICIES

When a client is truly serious about adopting a management style that encourages appropriate risk taking, one of the things we usually recommend is a change in hiring policies. We suggest looking for people who are not wedded to conventional business paradigms, people who may appear to be a bit radical for the prevailing atmosphere at the company but who possess vision and a willingness to try to bring that vision to life, if even it means that they might not succeed. Seek out those whose breadth of experience may indicate that they've taken an alternative or unique path to your door. The value of having people who are not carbon copies of the leader can't be overstated.

Before Michael Eisner became chairman and CEO of Disney in 1984, he spent eight years as president of Paramount Pictures, a period in which the studio had a string of hits and critical successes. Yet he was rejected for the top job at Paramount because he was thought to be "too child-like." In the years since, Paramount has had its share of successes while undergoing a couple of ownership changes. Its performance pales, however, in comparison to that turned in by Disney since the childlike Eisner took the helm.

There is little to be gained from empowering employees whose careers have been geared to obedience and suppressing their individuality as they moved politely and gingerly up the corporate ladder. If you want to banish the "it can't be done here" mentality, support employees who challenge those rules that threaten creativity and stifle imagination.

The leader who dares to take risks is often an outsider who doesn't feel constricted by the establishment's rules. Such divergence from the established norm is typical in the arts, and art history is full of examples of innovation prompting outrage among the mainstream. The French Impressionist Claude Monet, for instance, was ridiculed by the art establishment early in his career because his daring experimentation with bright color violated traditional artistic conventions.

It may seem odd to describe Walt Disney as an outsider, yet that is exactly what he was for many years in Hollywood. As the producer of cartoons, he was looked upon as small time, the supplier of filler material shown by movie houses before the "real" feature presentation came on. Even the special awards given him by the Academy of Motion Picture Arts and Sciences in the early 1930s were discounted as something of a public-relations ploy by the industry. Some thought that

Disney, with his reputation as a producer of "family" products, was being singled out to counter the accusations of immorality that then dogged the industry. Not until he received an Oscar for the full-length *Snow White and the Seven Dwarfs* did Hollywood bestow any real recognition on Disney.

Throughout his lifetime, Walt continued to maintain a distance from the moviemaking elite. He never used big-name stars in his pictures, nor did he invite them to lavish parties or Disneyland events. Walt also shunned deals with big-time agents. Early on, he established his own standards and went his own way.

THE SLEEPING GIANT IS REAWAKENED

When Walt Disney died in 1966, the spirit of adventure with which he had imbued his company seemed to die with him. For almost two decades, the company continued to revere the image of its founder, but the old spark and inspiration were missing. The movies that were made during this time were lackluster in content and poorly received at the box office. Disney World, Walt Disney's brainchild, did open in 1971, but Disneyland in California installed no new attractions, and the parks were not refurbished. Moreover, the cost of the EPCOT Center was a huge drain on profits, and attendance at the park was not living up to expectations.

"What would Walt have done?" became the most frequently heard question at company headquarters. Some employees said they felt that they were working for a dead man. Net income dropped 18 percent in 1982 and slid another 7 percent the following year. The Walt Disney Company, an American institution, was on a slippery slope, and with its low stock price reflecting the company's disarray, it became ripe for takeover by corporate raiders who were circling like vultures.

Enter Michael Eisner. With the backing of Roy E. Disney, Walt's nephew and the son of cofounder Roy O. Disney, Eisner came on board in 1984 as chairman and chief executive officer, with Frank Wells assuming the post of president. Both men won the blessing of the wealthy Bass brothers of

Fort Worth, Texas, who owned a sizable stake in the company. The support of the Bass family was crucial because it assured the team a significant period of time in which to rescue the foundering company without interference from outside investors.

Disney's legacy was now in the hands of men who understood how to run the company as Walt had done, and how to take calculated risks. It didn't take them long to rekindle the magic. New investment in feature-film animation and a string of live-action hits that reflected the tastes of contemporary movie-going audiences vaulted the company into the ranks of major movie studios, a place it had never occupied before. With the large-scale syndication of Disney's huge video library, the release of animated classics on videocassette, expansion and renovation at the theme parks (the whirlwind of activity was astonishing), Eisner and Wells managed to double Disney profits within two years. The duo had remade Disney into a company that dared to excel. Tragically, Wells died in a helicopter crash in 1994.

Along the way, Eisner and his management team have made some mistakes, to be sure, but they have always rectified them. Most important, they have worked to maintain the high standards that Walt Disney set for the parks and for the burgeoning list of Disney products.

That is not to say that every new movie has been an artistic and commercial success. Eisner admits that some releases have not measured up as he would like. For example, the movie *Tron,* released in 1982, was a box-office failure, but in true Disney fashion, it introduced more advanced technology that the company will be able to utilize in future films. "When you're trying to break ground creatively," Eisner says, "you do sometimes fall short. That's risk, and we try to manage it well."[20]

One of the company's great success stories in recent years has been the Disney stores. What began as theme-park shops where customers could buy Mickey Mouse tee shirts and other Disney memorabilia have expanded to include more than 600 retail outlets across the country, 101 of which were opened in 1996 in conjunction with the release of the movie *101 Dalmatians.*[21]

The idea to expand the company's retail presence into malls and shopping centers came from Disney employee Steve Burke. Originally, Eisner didn't much like Burke's suggestion, but he listened to the arguments and decided to give it a try. His willingness to take the risk has provided handsome returns: In 1997, the stores brought in more than $100 million in revenues.

That risk taking is alive and well at the Walt Disney Company is nowhere more apparent than in its dramatic entrance onto the Broadway stage. Disney's first foray, *Beauty and the Beast,* raised skepticism about the wisdom of transferring an animated film to live theater, but four years after its debut, the play still delights Broadway audiences. More recently, the highly acclaimed *The Lion King* has been setting Broadway records.

The opening of *The Lion King* represented bilevel risk taking for Disney. First, the company poured millions of dollars into renovating the dilapidated New Amsterdam Theater on New York's 42nd Street, helping the city to turn around a seedy neighborhood in the process. Then, the theatrical version of the movie musical was brought to life on the Amsterdam's stage. With its innovative staging and imaginative use of puppetry designed by its multitalented director, Julie Taymor, the production broke new ground in the long and glorious history of Broadway. One reviewer said that "as visual tapestry, there is nothing else like it."

Not surprisingly, the show instantly became an enormous hit, proving that the Walt Disney Company still dares to take risks, still dares to excel, and in doing so, still dares to provide sheer magic to its audiences.

Looking ahead to Chapter 8, we'll see how those who dare to take risks to further their dreams implement the final piece of the four-pillared Disney philosophy: Do. To make your dreams come true, you must know how to execute. It all begins with the right kind of training and orientation for every one of your cast members.

Questions to Ask
- Is your culture stuck in paradigms that are no longer effective for your business?

- Do you squelch long-term thinking in favor of short-term rewards?
- Do you avoid micromanagement of employees?
- Do you routinely give employees the opportunity to grow beyond their current responsibilities?
- Do you create an atmosphere where failures are accepted and analyzed for learning purposes and possible future innovation?
- Do you promote cross-functional teams for the purpose of reengineering outdated processes and procedures?

Actions to Take
- Grant employees the opportunity to develop and implement innovative ideas in all areas of their jobs: product, process, and service.
- Schedule off-site retreats and meetings to encourage breakthrough, risk-taking ideas that may fundamentally change the way you do business.
- Assign cross-functional teams to reengineer products, processes, and services. Examine projects that failed and celebrate employee efforts despite the outcome.
- Communicate to employees how the study of so-called "organizational failures" is essential for planning future projects and strategies.

THE SPIRIT OF CHALLENGE

When the Whirlpool Global No-Frost project started, Jerry McColgin was faced with a real challenge. Not only was the schedule cut by a third, but so was the budget. He thought he could deliver on time if—but only if—he had the team fully behind him. "I felt it was doable, but the team would tell me if I was right or not. I decided, for my benefit and for the team's benefit, that we had to decide very quickly. We couldn't get half-way through and then realize that we couldn't deliver. This was one of the main reasons I took everyone off for a five-day retreat. We all concluded that the project was feasible within the time and budget limits the company had given us."

Of course, by its very nature, the team took risks all along the way. Inviting the suppliers to work as partners was a major risk. Everyone involved was under a microscope from top management. Management had cooperated all the way—by setting up an international team, by giving the team specially outfitted and expensive offices, and by allowing personnel to be taken away from their regular functions to work full time with the team. All of these moves created some resentment and jealousy among coworkers.

The Global No-Frost team was always under pressure to reach its milestones on schedule. "From a risk point of view," says McColgin, "we were carrying a heavy load."

There were personal risks too. Take the case of the finance manager. When the project began, McColgin interviewed various people within the company and found no one he felt was really right. Then an American, who had been working as a controller in Brazil, came to see him. He wanted to relocate back to his own country. He was offered the job but expressed reservations at the risk involved in taking on a two-year job when he needed permanence. But he accepted the risk and took the job. In the end he was given a management position in the company.

PRACTICE, PRACTICE, PRACTICE

The growth and development of the Walt Disney Company is directly related to the growth and development of its human resources—our cast.[22]

WALT DISNEY

A ctors, musicians, athletes, and others who perform in public must train and practice. Otherwise, they risk embarrassing themselves and incurring the displeasure of spectators. Of great importance, too, is the teacher or coach who tells the musician that he's hitting the wrong notes or advises the athlete about batting stance, running form, and so on. Without such helpful criticism and the benefit of the more experienced mentor's knowledge, a performer's career is likely to be short-lived.

So it is in business. To perform at their best, a company's employees must be thoroughly trained, and they need the help of more experienced staff members. Moreover, to maintain their competencies, training can't be a one-shot thing; it must be ongoing.

Perhaps because of his background as an artist, Walt Disney fully understood the essential part that training and practice play in the development of an individual's talents. Add in his well-known penchant for perfection, and it's hardly surprising that he adamantly insisted on rigorous and continuous training for all of his "cast members." After all, common sense dictates that everyone, from the back-stage crew to the performers out front, must be thoroughly rehearsed in order to put on the really "good show." But like so much else at the company Walt built, training takes on a special quality not found at most other organizations. Disney even devotes an entire "university" to it.

The students of Disney University enjoy the most exciting campus of any educational institution in the country, the over 29,000 acres of Disneyland and Disney World and anywhere else the company operates. The required course work is brief, but it's famous for its intensity. The freshmen are all new members of the Disney family: Some are there to prepare for a summer job; others are being readied to assume a permanent position.

Disney University—a process, not an institution—was conceived by Walt Disney himself prior to the opening of Disneyland in the 1950s. Today, every new employee, from senior executives to part-time desk clerks and tour guides, is required to undergo training prior to embarking on her or his day-to-day responsibilities. And in typical Disney fashion, the training process leaves nothing to chance, imparting knowledge not only about specific job skills and competencies but also, and perhaps more important, ensuring that every employee has a thorough understanding of the Disney culture and traditions.

Thus, what is euphemistically called "human resources" at many organizations—which view training as no more than an expensive but sometimes necessary evil—is given top priority in the Disney universe. That's because Walt considered training an essential investment in the future of his company.

Obviously, not every organization has access to the facilities and resources that comprise Disney University, but every organization can adopt the attitude that underlies the Disney approach to training. In this chapter, we examine that attitude and help you distinguish between training that is purely perfunctory and the kind that will enable your employees to perform at their peak.

TRAINING—WHOSE RESPONSIBILITY IS IT?

Only two days after Disneyland opened on July 13, 1955, Walt Disney called the vice president of casting into his office. Normally the calmest of individuals, Disney was so upset over a situation at Tom Sawyer's Island that he shooed everyone but the casting executive out of his office and closed the door, an uncharacteristic act for Walt Disney.

The immediate cause of Disney's agitation was the behavior of the boy hired to play Tom Sawyer. The red-haired, freckle-faced 12-year-old, who greatly resembled the fictitious Missouri schoolboy, apparently had read Mark Twain's novel and was going to great lengths to imitate the rambunctious Tom: He was actually picking fights with other boys visiting the island!

It was a delicate matter, since Walt himself had suggested the boy, previously a messenger in his office, for the job. The vice president, taking his cue from the boss, had hired the young man on the spot. Now the executive was telling Disney, "The kid is beating up all your guests. We have to fire him."

But Walt's response, from behind closed doors, took the vice president by surprise. The boss was upset, to be sure, but his anger was directed toward the executive for *his failure to train the boy* to deliver the "good show." The youngster was only trying to do his job in the best way he knew how, Walt reasoned. The fault lay with Disney management for not making sure the boy understood what was expected of him.

The incident, which had been forgotten until it was recounted by the then-retired vice president at a celebration honoring the little red-haired boy for his 30 years of service to the company, illustrates the underlying belief that led to the evolution of Disney University into a world-class training program. Because Walt Disney believed so strongly in a company's responsibility for training its employees, students at Disney U now receive a complete orientation called Traditions, which includes an explanation of the company's values and traditions, on-the-job training, and procedures for advancement.

As the story suggests, Walt Disney understood the detrimental effects that the sink-or-swim mentality can have on the workplace. Under this approach, which unfortunately is prevalent at far too many companies today, people are thrown into new jobs and left to discover the rip tides on their own—hopefully before they are dragged under by them. If someone is deemed worthy of being in your employ, why not take the time to pilot him or her through dangerous currents? After all, if you buy a $30,000 piece of equipment, you would likely follow the manufacturers' break-in procedure.

Consider an orientation program as the recommended break-in procedure for new employees. Drawing on the expertise of its veterans, Disney designates trainers in each department to oversee and guide the work of new cast members. Frontline employees at Disney also serve as facilitators in some training sessions, sharing their on-the-job experiences with newcomers. Believing the adage that "to teach is to learn twice," Disney thus accomplishes the dual goal of instructing new staffers while reinforcing company values and traditions among old hands. Such contact with senior staffers also makes clear to new cast members that opportunities for advancement are available.

But perhaps the thing that most distinguishes the Disney training approach is its initial concentration on making each new employee feel as if his or her efforts will make a real difference to the company as a whole. As the head of training and development at Disney University says, "If we want new cast members to deliver Disney, that is, to exceed people's expectations, then for those first few days they're with us, our new people better feel that the company believes the same about them."[23]

New employees who are thoroughly grounded in what is expected of them and who believe that the company has confidence in their abilities will gain an amazing degree of self-assurance. Consequently, they will do their jobs much better right from the start, increasing their value to their employers.

WHAT KIND OF TRAINING?

A few years back, *Training Magazine* estimated that $48 billion was being spent annually on the training of 47.2 million employees who put in 1.5 billion hours on professional development. That's a lot of money and a lot of people, so it sounds pretty impressive until you begin to scrutinize the numbers carefully. The 47.2 million employees constituted only 37 percent of the workforce in the United States, while 54 percent of the money spent was allocated to training managerial candidates, who make up about 10 percent of the workforce. That's not such a splendid picture after all, and it gives rise to a number of questions:

- Are we training the right people?
- Are we getting the results we need to be competitive?
- Is standard training enough?
- What kind of training should be offered?

First and foremost, we must start training *all* employees, not just the professional managers. That many companies fail to grasp the urgency of implementing widespread training was brought home to us in our work with a client. This company had agreed to sponsor a program designed to teach both management and union employees how to improve performance. At the end of the third day, a mid-level manager came to us and said, "Why are you teaching these union employees management techniques?"

Somewhat taken aback by the question, we explained that we firmly believe that customer focus has to be everybody's job, but *especially* the frontline workers'. The misconception that only an elite group need be privy to a company's customer-focused mission, goals, and strategy presents a serious danger to any organization that buys into it. Without a doubt, such shortsightedness jeopardizes the company's achievement of its goals. For one thing, it deprives a company of a vast source of talent and ideas, and for another, it encourages a division among staff members that can only damage the organization.

To include everyone in training is a crucial first step, but to ensure that true learning will take place, an organization must also give every employee in a focused work environment an opportunity to use what has been taught. Lasting knowledge is acquired when on-the-job experience is used to reinforce what has been taught in the classroom.

Unfortunately, a great many companies employ the "spray and pray" method of training, that is, they spray training on people, then pray that they absorb it. That kind of slapdash approach is at odds with what we call the "Performance Learning Cycle," illustrated in Fig. 8-1, in which the depth of training is as important as the breadth. So all companies must ask themselves, "Are

FIGURE 8-1.   Performance Learning Cycle.

we giving our employees enough of the right kind of training?" That means providing employees with the techniques they need to achieve the desired customer-focused results and then following up with a hands-on situation that offers a chance to practice the ideas and learn from experience what works and what doesn't, all under the watchful eye of a veteran coach.

The next phases of the Performance Learning Cycle, after training and practice, are the measurement of achievement and its timely recognition. It almost goes without saying that recognizing and applauding an employee's contribution is critical to reinforcing the desired behavior. Without some expression of appreciation, the enthusiasm and hard work required for further improvement are likely to diminish. But someone who is commended for an achievement usually responds by producing even better results. Ultimately, the employer can expect that the results will translate into cost savings, quality improvements, reductions in cycle times, and strengthened customer relationships.

Appreciation means different things to different people, so how an organization chooses to recognize achievement depends on the circumstances involved and the culture of the organization. Disney uses various kinds of celebrations, service pins, distinguished service citations, and other internal excellence awards. A personal word of acknowledgment from a respected leader can go a long way, or small team rewards can help build morale—perhaps dinner at a restaurant or an informal office party. Monetary bonuses are always appropriate, of course, but when cash awards are not feasible, look for other forms of recognition.

When the newly learned skills are reinforced with coaching, practice, and recognition, they become habits, habits that will move your company steadily along the path of improvement. Moreover, a company that embraces employee training as an essential investment in its future will soon see that continuing education enhances the odds for sustained long-term success (Fig. 8-2).

To reap the optimum benefits of any training program, however, the entire company must be committed to it, with

FIGURE 8-2.   Habits.

the main push coming from the top. When it becomes clear that top management firmly supports the change effort, impressive results will follow.

When we first began to work with Plumbing & Industrial Supply, for example, the 38-member company had been trying for some time to implement a policy of total quality, but with minimal success. Among other things, multiple-day team retreats had been held to teach top management the new concepts, after which team members were supposed to relay what they had learned to the lower-level employees. Daily responsibilities required that the implementation be done piecemeal.

Our initial employee survey turned up a telling and disturbing attitude. The typical comment went something like this: "If the program is so important, then how come we're not really trained to do it? We're only getting a couple of hour-long sessions while management goes off for days." The snail's pace of implementation was clearly taking a toll.

Although we relayed the findings to management, we recognized that the company's small size was at the heart of the problem. Whereas a large company can afford to take groups of people off on retreat for three days without disrupting operations, that is not the case at a small company. So we suggested to the president that the training program be conducted on weekends. "Let people take one day off and then ask them to work overtime on Saturday or Sunday."

But the president had another solution: "There is no reason why you can't have three sessions of 10 or 12 people, and we [management] can take over their jobs while they are out. We can load trucks. We can drive their routes. It would probably be good for us to get back to the nitty-gritty jobs while the others are off being trained."[24]

Besides being an excellent sign of top-level commitment to the change program, the president's suggestion helped repair the breach that had opened between management and the workers, who had felt they were being treated like second-class citizens not worthy of training. Within a short time, total quality performance was successfully implemented throughout the organization.

MAKE EXCELLENCE A HABIT

The goal of learning is to develop positive habits that benefit individuals and organizations. When learning a foreign language, for example—say, Spanish—first a pupil studies to get good enough to understand and be understood in a social situation. That is a useful but limited skill. If that person goes to live in a Spanish-speaking country, his or her limited skill will at first prove inadequate for newfound needs. The language has to become like a habit, an involuntary reaction, before the student will be fully comfortable with it, but that won't happen until she has practiced, and then practiced some more.

Aristotle said, "We are what we repeatedly do...excellence, then, is not an act, but a habit."[25] If this is so, organizations that wish to pursue superior performance at all levels must work to ensure that the characteristics that define excellence are practiced, and then practiced some more, until they, too, become an involuntary reaction.

We believe that proper habits grow from obtaining knowledge, attitude, and skills. Knowledge is understanding what, how, and why we need to do something. Skill is applying that knowledge in a practical situation. Attitude is desiring to transform our knowledge into skills and, ultimately, into a habit. A company that claims the corporate value of excellence must therefore establish a specific ongoing process to transmit knowledge and, in turn, improve employees' skills.

But for such an effort to produce the desired results, a company must understand that the customer drives the process. Many times, we have encountered training programs for which an organization's human resources department has developed extensive in-depth material that neglects to mention the importance of the external customer. Employees are trained to refine their own skills and perhaps to take care of the needs of internal customers, but the *raison d'être,* the external customer who provides the revenues that support the company's existence, is ignored.

Knowledge of customer needs and expectations can be taught, but not attitude or motivation. These elements are transmitted through the behavioral patterns of employees and are part of the values and sense of mission that pervade the workplace. In fact, holocaust survivor Viktor Frankl defines *attitude* as "our response to what we have experienced."[26] The process is summarized in Fig. 8-3. That is why employee training becomes far more effective when old-timers, who can become role models as well as instructors, are involved. Their

FIGURE 8-3.   Attitude.

behaviors provide signals to new employees as to the company's underlying culture.

Illinois Power, which invested thought, money, and effort in developing a training program that supports its cultural transformation, exemplifies a company that has reaped the rewards of an organizationwide commitment to customer-focused training.

As an initial step in the implementation, we instituted an intensive training program that included a three-day Dream Retreat and a complete immersion in the concepts of total quality. The aim was to improve teamwork, customer service, and employee empowerment. In one small example, line workers were allowed to rearrange work schedules to allocate time more efficiently. By adopting a total quality initiative and making a point of training its employees in a "customer first" approach, Illinois Power instigated a remarkable turnaround throughout the company. Capping the utility's accomplishment was its 1991 receipt of its industry's most prestigious tribute, the Edison Award.

Another topflight company that has achieved enviable results with its training programs is Motorola. In the late 1980s, Motorola spent over $170 million on corporate education and was rewarded with sales of $6.7 billion. In 1997, Motorola sales reached nearly $30 billion, still more evidence of its employees' commitment to quality and "total customer satisfaction," its corporate objective.

As the decade of the 1970s drew to a close, management became increasingly aware that Japanese manufacturers were invading the company's markets with considerable success. And although Motorola was by no means in bad shape (profit improvement hovered between 5 and 10 percent per year), the CEO announced a five-year strategy designed to improve process, product, and sales. The measures put in motion included setting a strategic goal for quality (target of no more than 3.4 defects per million products); instituting performance rewards (savings stemming from team recommendations are shared as bonuses); initiating senior management reviews (constant reinvigoration of quality programs with results passing through the entire organization);

and most important, training employees (40 percent of training one year was devoted to quality matters.) The success of this creative combination has propelled Motorola to new heights.

BEWARE THE PERFORMANCE APPRAISAL

One of the favorite devices of human resources departments is the performance appraisal. These appraisals have become something of a constitutionally mandated fact of business management. We believe that these appraisals are, in truth, harmful to morale and unnecessarily costly for an organization to administer. Let us explain.

A few years ago, we asked the CEO of a major company what he considered his company's greatest asset. "My employees," he answered without hesitation. "I make certain that we hire the best possible people for the job." He then went on to explain his hiring policy, from the search process to the extensive interviewing of a candidate, the personality testing, and finally, the careful checking of references. It was an impressive list.

He concluded by saying, "My most important job is to make sure that my company is made up of winners."

When we asked him further about the company's performance appraisal system, he assured us that it, too, was carefully structured. Once a year, every employee was evaluated in depth by a supervisor, and the CEO was proud to report that supervisors spent a considerable amount of time and thought on performance appraisals.

Later on, we had the opportunity to chat with the supervisors and employees of the company. When we asked about performance appraisals, everyone, without exception, agreed that (1) performance appraisals were a waste of time; (2) people dreaded the entire ritual; (3) the process did not result in behavioral change; and (4) the outcome was influenced by the recentness of performance.

In the course of a year, we talk to hundreds of people, and the reaction to performance appraisals is universally negative. They are described as one of the biggest barriers to service and quality improvements. Here's why. Most people believe that they are above-average performers. When their appraisal evaluation rates them as average or below, they feel discouraged and misunderstood, and the quality of their work often suffers.

As the late W. Edwards Deming, considered the architect of total quality management, once described it:

> The effects are devastating. Such a system substitutes short-term performance for long-term planning, wrecks teamwork, and nurtures rivalry. It builds fear and leaves people bitter or despondent, unfit for work for weeks after receipt of the rating.[27]

Performance appraisals are highly subjective; they depend on the evaluator's personal attitudes. Suppose, for instance, that an employee has missed two days of work in the previous year. One supervisor might give relatively great weight to the absences, especially if the missed days have been recent, and rate the employee as "average," while another supervisor might completely ignore the missed days and assign an "excellent" rating.

Other factors, too, enter into the assessment of a worker, and they are often situations over which the individual has no control. For example, an employee may have the necessary education for a job and be a hard worker to boot, but further on-the-job training may be needed for the person to perform at the desired level. Some people are hired for jobs for which they do not have the appropriate education; others are evaluated on results that are heavily dependent on factors over which they have no control. Effort and commitment are really the only parts of the equation over which an employee has complete control, but it is impossible to isolate the effects of these factors.

In the final analysis, performance reviews may tempt a worker to try to please the boss at the expense either of fellow workers or, more important, the customer. Such efforts can undermine teamwork as well as job performance.

THERE IS A BETTER WAY

What are the alternatives to traditional performance appraisals? We help companies devise individual development plans that foster an environment of understanding and a commitment to personal growth. If you think about it, the word *development* sends a much more positive message within a company than does the term *appraisal*. A company that wants its workforce to be productive—and what company doesn't?— will find that individual development plans are more conducive to achieving that goal.

When creating personal development plans, the first requirement is that each employee understands the company's vision and its values and how they relate to the individual's responsibilities. Job scope and guidelines for performance must be clarified. Everyone from the mailroom employee, whose speedy and accurate job performance precludes stopping to chat at every office, to the middle manager, whose in-box should be emptied expeditiously, must understand his or her part in the process. It should be made clear that one person's failure to carry out assigned duties has an impact on the whole process and that the organization is only as strong as its weakest link.

One of our clients took an interesting approach to developing guidelines for employees. Rather than defining procedures, the company identified areas of known failure, ideas that had been tried in the past without success. Other than these particular paths, employees were free to exercise their own initiative in order to obtain desired results. Having an understanding of how and why something failed in the past enabled the employees to accomplish their goals more efficiently. With this example in mind, we encourage our clients to go heavy on guidelines and light on procedures, particularly when training employees.

A second imperative for setting up effective development plans is that desired outcomes be jointly defined by management and employees. Avoid specifying methods and means. Doing so only leads to undesirable and unproductive micromanagement.

What's more, tightly prescribed approaches give employees a built-in excuse for failure; for example, "I did what you told me to do, so it's not my fault if something went wrong." Often a simple example of what quality output looks like is the best motivator. At the moment of understanding, all those necessary measurable objectives and expected results will make sense to them.

At Disneyland, Jungle Boat cast members are given a script that suggests telling certain jokes but still allows cruise leaders to inject their own personalities into the performance. By giving cast members guidelines rather than dictates with prescribed expectations for the outcome, the Walt Disney Company is encouraging employees to exercise good judgment, which is a hallmark of empowerment.

A third area of importance in designing individual development plans is an evaluation of processes. According to sociologist Kurt Lewin, effectively changing behavior requires consideration of the environment and the process as well as the person. "Behavior," he observed, "is a function of the person times the environment."[28]

An experience at a former client illustrates the validity of Lewin's observation. The company, which made automobile engine parts, had a milling plant staffed by good but not exceptional workers. Everything went along fine most of the time, but occasionally, product quality levels would drop into the unacceptable range for no apparent reason. During one of these dips, the company's human resources department decided that the plant workers' attitude was at fault. So HR launched a comprehensive training program in interpersonal relationships. Alas, the quality levels did not change. Why? Because this approach wrongly assumed that change comes solely from the individual. In this particular case, further investigation revealed that the quality discrepancies were the result of problems at the raw materials supplier. Deming validates Lewin's concept. He once stated that more than 85 percent of the United States quality and productivity problems are the result of the process. Therefore, it is imperative that process improvements be discussed between management and employees. Process improvements may also require changes in management policy. Management needs to assume a proactive role by asking the following questions:

- What do you need from management to reach your objectives?
- How can we both achieve great success?
- How can we remove barriers to success?

Direct face-to-face discussion is key to evaluating the process correctly; contact via memos or e-mail will not ensure that the message is heard and absorbed on both ends. What's more, this dialogue must be ongoing to support continuous improvement.

Finally, personal development plans must include a determination of the positive and negative consequences associated with meeting or not meeting the desired results.

Although the plans should be revisited approximately every six months, or at the least on an annual basis, this activity is not a replacement for regular feedback. We encourage our clients to employ a 360-degree feedback system, such as our own *Vision 360,®* that constantly updates performance information. Immediate feedback provides the basis for achieving and maintaining excellence because it allows an organization to customize individual development plans. When everyone is helped to achieve personal bests (as described in Chapter 3, these must be aligned with the overall vision of the organization), the organization's overall performance improves dramatically.

As should be obvious by now, an organization's management cannot afford simply to say to new employees, "Here's what we expect of you. Now go to it." A company must be prepared to work with new employees and guide them until they become familiar with their responsibilities and the organization's culture. The former manager of customer satisfaction at Disney summed up the reasons for Disney's success this way:

> Recruit the right people, train them, continually communicate
> with them, ask their opinions, involve them, recognize them,
> and celebrate with them. If you show respect for their opinions
> and involvement, they will be proud of what they do and they'll
> deliver quality service.[29]

Nothing more need be said. With all employees primed to deliver, we will take a look next at the role proper planning plays in bringing dreams to fruition.

Questions to Ask
- Do you support individual development planning rather than the demoralizing performance appraisal?
- Do you verbalize and demonstrate to employees that you value their partnership in creating plans for their own self development?
- Are you providing training to the right people in the organization?
- Do you provide training that is tailored to the needs of your employees?
- Do you celebrate the contributions of employees, even when they are not exactly in line with management's thinking?
- Do your managers coach employees to reinforce important concepts after they have been formally trained?

Actions to Take
- Ask for feedback from employees on the value of specific organizational training that they attend.
- Concentrate training efforts on those who need skill development rather than on those who desire training as a company perk.
- Schedule follow-up sessions with employees to reinforce skills learned in a formal training environment.
- Ask employees to engage in regular 360-degree evaluations.
- Institute development plans in place of performance appraisals. Work in partnership with employees to create their own plans.

WORK HARD, PLAY HARD

All the members of the Global No-Frost team were experts in their fields, but many were philosophically far removed from a culture that endorses teamwork. It isn't easy, we have discovered in our consulting work, for people who are used to working within a hierarchical, conservative structure to adjust to a completely different work environment. Describing his experiences throughout the project, Jerry said, "I could see people's expectations grow and grow and grow. They were pushing themselves on all levels." In the end, people said that they had never felt so fulfilled, so satisfied by any job.

One situation that Jerry faced involved the cultural differences between team members. Even though everyone had a sense of commonality about the work, there were nevertheless differences of behavior and attitude. So we initiated another two-day session for the team and called in two professional advisors to enlighten us about national differences. They warned the non-Americans that Americans could be brash, sarcastic, and loud. Then they warned Americans that Indians and other Asians often hold back, watching and waiting for signals from their superiors before they contribute anything. On the other hand, Brazilians, they said, can be argumentative and noisy. Gradually, we established what you might call cultural assimilation, a trained awareness and respect for national differences. It was still a gradual process, but knowing what to expect from another member often smoothed the way. It kept people from being offended and created an empathy that continued to grow throughout the process.

Jerry also felt that he didn't just want his team members to know each other only on a nine-to-five basis. To foster the sense of a team identity, he organized after-work events. "Fairly early on, we developed a work hard and play hard environment," he explains, "lots of parties involving families. We had barbecues, cookouts, and trips to local fairs."

There were more formal celebrations, too, when a milestone was met, but these were on company time and at company expense. The impromptu gatherings were more family affairs and really served to establish cross-cultural bonds.

MAKE YOUR ELEPHANT FLY— PLAN

On this and every turn, we'll be making progress and progress is not just moving ahead. Progress is dreaming, working, building a better way of life.[30]

WALT DISNEY

Vision without a means of execution is like a plane without wings or Dumbo without his ears—it just won't fly. No matter how deep a company's resources are, progress of company projects greatly depends on the strength of execution, and proper execution requires thorough and detailed planning, a reality that Walt Disney understood completely.

No wand-waving or intonations of "abracadabra" preceded the building of Disney's Magic Kingdom. The cartoons, movies, theme parks, and all the rest of the delights that took shape in Walt's prolific imagination came into being through a precise process of planning that he employed from the very beginning of his career. Making a movie is a costly undertaking, but because animation is especially expensive and labor-intensive, Disney *had* to plan carefully to control costs and successfully execute his ideas. Out of necessity was born a nine-step process that takes a "blue sky" idea and turns it into reality.

Dumbo, the perennial animated favorite about the flying baby elephant, was itself a product of this rigorous Disney regimen. By putting process in creativity—in this case, using a straightforward script and story and resisting the temptation to experiment with expensive new technologies—Disney and his animators produced *Dumbo* in just one year. As one Disney executive has described it, the system says, in effect, "Within these boundaries you will create. This is the budget, these are the limitations. Make it work within this framework."[31]

And work it has, as consistently successful and profitable flights of fancy from *Dumbo* to *Aladdin* attest. While our clients may not be staging magic carpet rides, we have seen diverse companies devise their own methods, both formal and informal, to ensure that a workable idea will actually come to fruition. In this chapter, we look at both the Disney "blue sky" process and the variations crafted by companies in a range of industries.

CAREFULLY MANAGED CREATIVITY, THE DISNEY WAY

There have always been two basic schools of thought on business creativity. The first insists that researchers and other in-house innovators be given the loosest rein possible, allowing new ideas and projects to develop on their own momentum with a maximum of independent decision making. The second approach demands that the reins be kept taut, that the generation of ideas be part of the corporate process, and like the other parts, that it be carefully managed.

Walt Disney was definitely of the second school. Although his famously forceful and controlling management style was largely attributable to his personality, there was also a practical consideration, the cost of making animated pictures. Makers of live-action films could shoot extra footage and then piece together their final product through artful cutting in the editing room, but animation costs were such that cartoon makers couldn't even consider this whittle-down approach.

So to keep costs in check, Disney exercised extremely tight control of the creative process itself by instituting a rigorous, nine-step regimen for project management. Only by demanding that his people follow this standard procedure could he continue to turn dreams into tangible products, whether he was dealing with films, amusement parks, television shows, or any of the other Disney enterprises. In the Disney system, nothing was—or is—left to chance. Figure 9-1 illustrates the planning process.

In schematic form, the process looks like this.

Step 1—Blue sky

- Ask "what if?" rather than "what?"
- Learn to live for a time with the discomfort of not knowing, of not being in full control.
- Take a trip through fantasyland; start with the story.

Step 2—Concept development

- Develop research.
- Evaluate alternatives.
- Recommend an idea.

Step 3—Feasibility

- Reconcile scope.
- Prepare pro forma.

Planning Guidelines

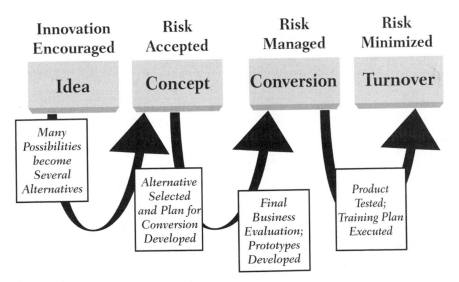

FIGURE 9-1. Planning guidelines.

Step 4—Schematic

- Finalize master plan.
- Outline initial business processes.

Step 5—Design objectives

- Finalize design details, equipment, and materials.
- Develop implementation strategy and budget.

Step 6—Contract documents

- Prepare contract documents.

Step 7—Production

- Construct site infrastructure and develop work areas.
- Produce show elements.

Step 8—Install, test, adjust

- Install the show.

Step 9—Close out

- Assemble final project documents.
- Monitor performance.
- Get sign-off letter from operations.

We like to add a Step 10: Celebrate a job well done!

Although managers at many companies fly by the seat of their pants, Disney executives follow these guidelines for aligning the company's long-term vision with short-term execution. Not only is the company kept on track from project to project, but costs are cut and production is speeded. Such strict adherence to a set of production standards and processes enables Disney to deliver consistently successful products and services.

THE PROCESS IN PRACTICE

New technology of every kind intrigued Walt Disney, but railroading held a special fascination for him. So when he could finally afford it, he built his own miniature train on his Holmby Hills estate. He spent hours driving it around, dreaming and planning. So when the time came to build Disneyland, it was only logical that Disney would be drawn to the idea of installing a monorail. Because Disney's single-track vehicle was the first ever built in the United States, there weren't any American engineers with the knowledge or training to construct it. So Disney turned to German engineers to help with the job.

When the monorail was completed at the end of six months, the Germans congratulated him on the amazing accomplishment. What had taken six or seven years to build in Germany had been finished in only half a year by Walt Disney. The Disneyland monorail represented planning and execution at its best.

Before planning or execution, of course, must come the vision. Without a vision, or "story" as discussed in Chapter 2, there is nothing to plan. The first step, then, is the generation of new ideas, ideas designed to satisfy customer needs or solve customer problems. A team must be prepared to suggest, discuss, argue about, and try out any number of diverse ideas. If one or more ideas fail, no real harm is done. We remind the teams we work with that although Babe Ruth hit 714 home runs, he also struck out 1330 times. So striking out a few times doesn't stop someone from eventually setting a record.

Trying out ideas, perhaps putting parts of several ideas together to produce a prototype, helps develop an overall concept and determine whether or not it is workable. A prototype can be evaluated and market tested, and it can serve as the centerpiece around which the process is developed.

When Lee Iacocca came up with the idea of reintroducing convertibles into the Chrysler product line, he began by asking his engineers to make him a prototype. After some figuring, the engineers came back and told him they could do it, but it would take nine months. The exasperated Iacocca, wondering why a prototype of what he had in mind should take so long to make, responded in effect: "You just don't understand. Go find a car and saw the top off the damn thing!" Within a few days, Iacocca had his convertible, which he then drove around Detroit, conducting his own version of a marketing study. People stopped and waved at him, shouted encouragement, or just turned and stared in wonder. Iacocca counted the stares, the shouts, and the waves that his prototype convertible elicited. After he had received a certain number of these responses, he decided that Chrysler should go ahead with a line of convertibles.

In some ways, the vision and idea-generation steps are among the simpler parts of the project-management process. Any number of people can sit around a corporate conference table and spin out a set of ideas and objectives for their company. The real difficulty is in determining how to go about reaching those goals.

Implementation of a project demands a carefully thought out structure that establishes specific guidelines, from the initial "blue sky" idea up to the final stages of completion. Certain milestones along the way must be specified, points at which management is appraised of overall progress. Those who work on a project need to know what is required at each step and how to measure their headway. Efficiency dictates that nothing be left to chance. Barring unforeseen acts of God, managers carefully plot every step on the chosen path.

We recognize that in today's business climate, a forceful ruler patterned after Walt Disney might generate no small amount of enmity and have a harder time maintaining control, particularly if the company involved has a somewhat freewheeling culture. And in fact, a strong argument can be made for giving creative minds the maximum amount of freedom. But most companies find that an approach that falls somewhere between absolute control and complete freedom works best for them.

We recommend that each company design its own procedures for turning a dream into reality. Such a process works best if it grows naturally out of discussions among management and employees rather than being imposed from the outside. That way, it can more adequately reflect the company's culture, history, traditions, and structure.

Many of our clients have successfully adopted rigorous processes similar to the Disney approach but tailored to manufacturing and service businesses. At one company, for example, the first phase is called the *Idea*.

In screening the Idea, the company initially asks:

- What is the compelling customer benefit?
- How is the idea going to increase shareholder value?
- Does it fit strategically into the organization?
- What resources are required to move the idea into the next phase?

Next comes the *Concept* phase. The questions asked at this stage include:

- What is the market assessment?
- Is the concept technically feasible?
- What is the business analysis?
- What are the preliminary design specifications?
- What plans and resources are required to move to the third phase?

The third stage is *Conversion.* Here the questions are:

- What is the business case?
- What critical process and product elements can we identify?
- What is the plan of execution, and how can we make it happen?
- What costs and benefits will be associated with the final phase?

And, as the company moves into the final *Execution* phase, it asks:

- How do we release the product (if there is one)?
- When is the process going to be implemented?
- How do we get the product to the customer?
- Do we have a feedback mechanism in place to gauge the success of the product?

With carefully determined guidelines and milestones, teams or departments can proceed on their own. Micromanagement is avoided because the company does not have to keep track of what everyone is doing every minute of the day. There is no need to ask how the project is going." Instead, management can safely trust that the team is keeping tabs on progress and that appropriate appraisals will be forthcoming at specified points along the way.

Project leaders understand, of course, that if problems arise which threaten deadlines or if some assistance is needed, management is there to help. Otherwise, the message from management should be, "You're on your own until you've finished this phase of the project." An interesting sidelight about Disney's planning process is that many times a project may not receive the necessary funding to continue. In most companies, when this happens, the team is viewed as a failure. At Disney, they look at these projects as assets that may be dusted off and continued midstream as funding or technology becomes available.

A PLANNING CENTER FACILITATES COMMUNICATION

One of the most effective tools we've found for managing a project and bringing an idea to its successful fruition is a planning center, a room where all the various elements of an entire project and its progress can be assembled.

When the Walt Disney Company was still small—some 1200 employees—management pinned rough drafts of drawings and story ideas to the walls of a planning room so that the exact status of a project could be quickly ascertained. Walt Disney didn't care much for meetings or written reports. He preferred to wander into the planning center alone, usually late at night, and scan the walls for samples of work in progress. Comparing the visuals to the vision he held in his mind told him instantly whether a cartoon or feature film project was on the right track.

A similar type of planning center was established when we worked with a large South African company that had 54 plants throughout the country. The complex assignment involved installing a materials management system over a three-year period. The first step was to figure out how to manage the relevant mass of material. Borrowing from Pentagon jargon, a "war room" was set up that allowed the project team to keep abreast of what was going on and where. The room was approximately 25 feet by 35 feet, with 15-foot-high walls where information could be displayed. So as not to waste valuable space, the room was windowless.

On one wall were pinned the plans for the project, which enabled everyone to know at a glance when training would start, when the software would arrive, when the next general meeting was to take place. A special section of the planning wall was reserved for messages. This became the communications center. We have found that although people often ignore e-mail and telephone messages, somehow it's harder to ignore a message when it's printed on a card and openly displayed. Perhaps the public nature of such communication makes it more difficult to disregard.

Another wall of the center was dedicated to keeping everyone up to date on what other team members were working on and how far along their individual pieces of the project were. When a segment was completed, that fact was posted in a special section. Another place was set aside for anyone who had a problem. The project manager could walk in and see immediately what difficulties lay ahead, then take the appropriate action. If someone was having trouble getting accounting department approval of a costing method, for example, the manager could step in and move the process along.

Occasionally, people who are greatly attached to their computer system complain that all plans can be tracked online. "Why do we need a visual display?" they ask.

The whole point of a planning center is to allow people to see a holistic picture of the projects and activities throughout the organization. What's more, when two or three people congregate in an area where the significant work of the company is visually displayed, often an impromptu meeting takes place. People communicate better face-to-face, and as discussed in Chapter 5, MIT research supports this conclusion. The quality of communication improves markedly with proximity. Close contact encourages questions and discussion, which is the kind of interaction needed to move projects along.

The planning center proved to be a valuable tool for a team we know that ran a testing laboratory. Any team member could walk in and scan the wall for information on all of the company's major projects and their stage of development. If the head of the testing lab noticed, for example, that one department was experimenting with a new product, he could be pretty certain that sooner or later his lab would be asked to perform certain tests. Previously, he probably would have received an unexpected call saying, "Hey, tomorrow I'm going to be sending you a part, and I need 47 tests done on it right away."

The new information alerted the lab manager to find out approximately when the work might arrive so that he could schedule someone to be ready to do the testing. For the first time, the engineering and the lab staffs were working together in a meaningful and cooperative manner.

Unexpectedly, the planning center also turned into a morale builder. It brought employees together and gave them a sense of involvement in all aspects of the company's processes. People began to feel that they had a voice in developments outside their own department. Compartmentalization gradually disappeared.

Planning centers are useful when working on side issues within projects—or projects within projects. One client's cross-functional team was charged with evaluating internal planning barriers and developing solutions which would promote buy-in from all stakeholders in the main project. The symptoms, or "pain," as we call it, were pretty clear from the start: Many people were angry about being left out of the planning and communication loops on a project which required their input in order to be successful.

The planning center is a practical approach for targeting the status of any one of the myriad pieces in a company process or for viewing the overall picture. The physical size of the center and the breadth of information displayed can vary, of course, according to specific needs. All that matters is that project leaders and participants have a way of keeping abreast of individual and overall goals, specific progress toward those goals, and any problems or needs encountered at various stages of a project.

Another form of the planning center is embodied in the concept of colocating, which we discussed previously in conjunction with teaming. When the Whirlpool technology team decided to colocate people from around the world to work in its Evansville, Indiana, facility, a subteam was charged with coordinating the colocation activities. To facilitate small-group interaction, the subteam's leader went to great lengths to create just the right environment.

This leader worked closely with two furniture suppliers to put together smaller functional areas within the total space allocated for the entire team. He also installed an active noise system that effectively tripled the perceived distance between individual team members in terms of the privacy it created. In the case of this Whirlpool global team, the illusion of greater distance was particularly important because many of the team members had a difficult time adjusting to the open-room style. In addition, the multiple languages spoken by the participants made the system imperative. Since people tend to listen when others speak a different language, it would have been virtually impossible for group members to tune out each other's conversations.

The effort involved in putting together the colocation space paid off for the Whirlpool team, which put together and executed a project that ended up surpassing everyone's expectations. The ease of communication that both planning centers and colocating promote goes a long way toward keeping a project on track and ensuring its ultimate success.

TAKING THE HOLISTIC APPROACH

How do you make your elephant fly when your business is far removed from the world of animation? John Dunn has been very successful in putting wings on his hotel-management operation by aligning long-term vision with short-term execution. Using a few simple but powerful techniques, Dunn has brought his vision of customer-focused service from the conceptual stage to the celebration stage for a job well done. And in doing so, he has also managed to integrate the geographically diverse parts of his midwestern organization into a smoothly functioning whole.

What we particularly like about Dunn's process is his personalized, idiosyncratic feedback mechanism. Just like Michael Eisner and Walt Disney before him, Dunn makes sure that he witnesses employee performance firsthand, and he has devised a novel approach for doing so.

The first thing Dunn did was to craft a mission statement that clearly states the company's "customers first" policy. Then he made sure that everyone in his company, from vice presidents to bellhops, learned it and understood it. All employees are expected to carry a pocket card bearing the mission statement with them at all times. When Dunn visits one of his properties, he frequently asks a staff member to show him the card bearing the statement. If the card is produced, the employee receives a $5 bill on the spot. Those who can recite the mission statement when asked—it doesn't have to be word perfect—get another $15.

As frequent visitors to his hotels, we can attest to the success of John's method. One day we were having lunch with John when we decided to test the effectiveness of his approach on our waitress. A few questions turned up the fact that she had been a Dunn Hospitality employee for only three weeks, but when we asked to see her mission card, she eagerly and proudly pulled it out of her pocket. When asked to recite the company's mission, she didn't miss a beat. Needless to say, John was beaming as he surprised her by handing her a $20 bill.

Dunn's training of new staff members is renowned for its thoroughness. The program, which takes up to two weeks, covers every detail of an employee's job. The company insists that customers come first, before any other employee, even before John Dunn himself. One new staffer who had worked in other hotels told us that he was astonished by the intensity of the training and by the commitment to the mission that it generates among employees at every level. All employees now think holistically in terms of what they can do to advance the company's goals, not in terms of what might work best for their individual fiefdoms. By allowing customer focus to drive the company, Dunn has broken down the barriers between management and staff and between the individual internal functions.

Thinking holistically is counterintuitive for those schooled in the principles of corporate Darwinism, where only the so-called fittest survive and where the law of the jungle guides most decision making. To overcome those blocks and to help people accustom themselves to the concept of the holistic company—where everyone works for the common good of the organization, we conduct an exercise in which clients sit in groups of five at separate tables. We hand each person an envelope with pieces of a puzzle. The goal is for all players to finish their puzzles, but to succeed, they have to trade pieces without saying a word.

This is not a competition, but as the game progresses, invariably some players begin to compete, hoard pieces, and strive to finish their own puzzles—and their group's—before anyone else does. After the experience, the participants who have pitted themselves against one another begin to understand that success comes from not hoarding pieces, either individually or within a group. The fastest way to win—for all players to finish their puzzles—is for everyone to collaborate across "organizational" boundaries, in other words, to think and to act holistically.

As you set about using the tools described in this chapter to design your own planning procedures, we must add one word of caution. Don't get so involved with making plans that they become the be-all and end-all. Some teams are so proud of the fine plans they craft that they forget about implementing them. They begin to look at the plan as their deliverable. Get in the habit of thinking *execution* immediately after you say the word *planning*.

One way to help you keep the process in perspective is through your system of rewards. Set it up so that idea generation is rewarded, to be sure, but save the biggest rewards and the largest celebration for the successful completion of the overall project. That way, employees will be encouraged to keep their eye on the ultimate goal.

That objective will be closer to your reach after you master the storyboarding technique that we will describe in the next chapter. Using it has helped our clients to conquer seemingly insoluble planning and communication problems. Once you learn how to storyboard, you will find it useful in solving a range of problems.

Questions to Ask

- Do organizational boundaries inhibit your planning processes?

- Do you have one or more planning centers in your organization where leaders and employees can work together on processes and projects?

- Do you have a designated communications center where employees can post their project timelines and critical aspects of their projects?

- Does your organization have a specific process for project implementation?

- Do you encourage the development of prototypes to help develop an overall concept and determine whether or not it is workable?

- Do you avoid micromanaging employees who are working on projects and champion their adherence to determining guidelines and milestones?

- Do you celebrate specific milestones and the completion of projects?

Actions to Take

- Develop a process for project implementation that is used throughout the company; provide training on the process and champion its use.

- Create planning and communication centers for project and process activities.

- Allow individuals and teams the flexibility to work on projects without management interference.

- Set up cross-functional project teams on a routine basis.

- Develop quick and inexpensive prototypes to test products, processes, or service ideas.

A NEW LEADERSHIP

We were really enlightened by the Global No-Frost team for a number of reasons. We often work in conservative situations where we cannot really experiment or try new approaches. This team gave us the chance to do just that, and in Jerry McColgin we found the ideal team leader. He understood his role.

Right from the start he announced that although he was the leader, hierarchy meant little to him. "I'm not going to sit in a closed office, and no one is forbidden to come in to see me. I want to hear from anyone who has a concern, a problem, or an issue." As he says himself, "I tend to be a proactive, risk-taking, cheerleading, inspirational type. Facts and do-it-by-the-book are not my way of working." His personal experiences working in amateur theatricals and on charity drives had also taught him how to lead groups of people. He realized early on that the team offered an extraordinarily high level of capacity, and he came to realize that his job was to harness these talents and to guide and direct them. He was not there to design a refrigerator; the engineers and designers could do that. In other words, Jerry understood that he was macromanaging the team, not micromanaging it. As long as the milestones were reached, he could preside and guide, leaving the details to his competent staff.

Very early on, at the first retreat, Jerry made a speech that was very influential in laying out the fundamentals of teamwork. Every individual at Whirlpool goes through an objective appraisal process which determines future raises and the size of the year-end bonus. The team would work by a different norm. Each member would be judged not on individual achievement but as part of a team, holistically. "I pointed to the marketing guy," Jerry remembers, "and said, 'You will only succeed if the manufacturing guy gets the equipment designed on time.' To the purchasing guy, I said, 'You will succeed only if the performance of the air-flow system is up to par.'" Jerry's message was that the success of the team depended on the sum of its parts—everyone working together at the highest level possible.

During the early retreat, the team began using storyboards to develop an entire 18-month plan so that people could see what had to be done and could negotiate their schedules. Someone said, "This is January and you expect me to get this done by April. I can't do this unless engineering produces its blueprints for this part by mid-March. I'm dependent on them. How can I do this?" With these kinds of comments, we walked through the whole process and established everyone's role and when they had to deliver a certain part of their output.

CAPTURE THE MAGIC WITH STORYBOARDS

Layer upon layer, we create a patchwork of sketches and words that color the original idea. Funny, fantastic, diverting, enhancing, persuasive, serious or not, our visualized thoughts begin to chisel away and uncover the diamond in the rough.[32]

DISNEY IMAGINEERS

Like many ingenious concepts, storyboarding takes a simple technique—visual display—and uses it in a unique way to help companies solve complex business problems. It is a structured exercise designed to capture the thoughts and ideas from a group of participants. Their thoughts and ideas are put on cards and then displayed on a board or a wall. The result, an "idea landscape," is more organized than the output from brainstorming, yet it retains the flexibility that project teams need as they work their way through the various stages of problem solving and idea generation.

Walt Disney originally conceived the idea that eventually became known as storyboarding as a way to keep track of the thousands of drawings necessary to achieve full animation of cartoon features. By having his artists pin their drawings in sequential order on the studio wall, Disney could quickly see which parts of a project were or were not completed.

From its genesis in animation, the technique has spread to many other areas. Advertising agencies now use storyboarding to sketch out commercials before they shoot them. Scenes from feature movies are often storyboarded for the next day's camera work. Editors and art directors utilize storyboards as a tool in producing picture books. It allows them to visualize what the final page will look like and to make sure that one page leads logically to the next.

But storyboarding is not limited to artistic endeavors. We suggest to companies that storyboarding is an effective method to conceptualize their mission statements, to develop best practices for manufacturing control systems, and to produce technical plans for improvements. Posted ideas or suggestions become the first step in the analysis of barriers, the investigation of their root causes, and the creation of team solutions. Any process can be mapped out in this way.

Storyboarding is a creative and efficient method for generating solutions to complex problems—those that can sometimes feel overwhelming—because it breaks situations into smaller, more manageable parts and focuses group attention on specific aspects of a problem. When ideas and suggestions are displayed on a wall where they can be read by all and moved about as storyboarding participants see fit, the confusion that can stymie breakthrough ideas is dissipated.

No other planning technique offers the flexibility of storyboarding. In this chapter, we explain exactly how storyboarding works, and we look at a number of examples of the technique in action. As you read how companies in various settings are successfully using it to solve a range of problems, think about putting the technique to work for your organization.

THE BIRTH OF A TECHNIQUE

When Walt Disney came up with the forerunner to the storyboarding technique in 1928, cartoon animation bore faint resemblance to the complex web of movement and color we know today. Full animation of cartoon features was still just a dream, but it was one Disney was striving to realize. To that end, he produced thousands more drawings than state-of-the-art animation required at that time.

The finished drawings were arranged in piles according to a predetermined narrative sequence. Then the cameraperson would photograph them, and the staff could watch them in a screening room. But with the prodigious output of drawings, it didn't take long before piles were stacked up in the studio. To bring some sense of order and to make it easier to follow a film's developing story line, Disney instructed his artists to display their drawings on a large piece of fiberboard that measured about four feet by eight feet.

Not just finished drawings but early rough sketches were pinned on the board. If there were problems with the story line or if a character wasn't taking shape as Disney wanted, changes could be made before the expensive work of animation was begun. The storyboard made it possible for Disney to experiment, to move drawings around, to change direction, to insert something he thought was missing, or to discard a sequence that wasn't working. And he could do all this *before* the animator had spent countless hours painstakingly putting in the final details.

Decades later, in the 1960s, the display technique was picked up by Disney's employee development program when the staff recognized its value for generating solutions to problems and enhancing communications in other areas. The refined storyboard concept has since been adapted to a variety of problem-solving situations in which the introduction of the visual element makes interconnections more readily apparent. As the participants pin cards to the wall, the team begins to develop various alternatives to solving the problem at hand.

Why doesn't a flip chart on an easel, a method often used in brainstorming sessions, work as well as a storyboard? On a flip chart, participants can see only one step at a time and therefore fail to get an overall picture. Moreover, flip charts can quickly become virtually unreadable as new ideas are inserted, old ideas are scratched out or moved around, and large arrows are left pointing nowhere. In addition, the lack of anonymity in brainstorming—participants must voice their ideas publicly—contributes a certain unease that discourages contributions. Our experience with both storyboarding and brainstorming allows us to make concrete comparisons in this regard: Whereas a 60-minute brainstorming session with 14 participants produces, on average, 42 utterances (questions, ideas, or comments), a storyboard session of the same size and duration typically produces anywhere from 150 to 300 utterances! Our studies have shown that in a typical fourteen-person brainstorming session, five participants produce 80 percent of the utterances, five participants produce 20 percent of the utterances, and the remaining four participants are observers of the meeting. In a storyboard session, all members of the group are active participants.

Anyone who has participated in the traditional, inefficient problem-solving meeting knows the drudgery of endless discussion, time-wasting repetitions, and lengthy explanations. Since only one person can talk at a time, most people's minds wander from the topic being discussed to the job waiting for them back at their desks. And invariably, a single participant tends to dominate the discussion. When the meeting finally drones to a close, it is virtually impossible to remember much of what was said.

Storyboarding, however, works to reverse this outcome. It is a fully participatory activity that places the entire sequence of a project, a company policy, or plan of action clearly in everyone's line of sight.

OVERCOMING SKEPTICISM

We generally acquaint clients with the concept of storyboarding early in our association. Even though we emphasize its enormous value, acceptance is not a foregone conclusion. The idea of congregating around a space decorated with rows of cards on the wall seems totally outlandish to people who have never witnessed a storyboarding session.

A utility that we worked with in Indianapolis, for example, had spent almost two years trying to devise a plan for implementing total quality. After untold hours of management meetings, brainstorming, and arguing, the executive team still couldn't agree on a plan. When we arrived with a stack of cards and dozens of markers, the group listened politely as we explained storyboarding, but they were clearly dubious about the whole approach. Nevertheless, they agreed to give it a try.

The group appeared far from convinced at the outset of our session that tacking cards on a wall would do anything to solve those problems that had baffled them for two years. We began by asking them for their ideas for potential solutions, which they wrote out and we put up on the board. As the cards were moved around and new ideas added, a structure for their implementation plans gradually developed.

The storyboarding process is like building a house; it entails a logical progression. Just as a house begins with the architect's conceptual rendering and then moves through the various stages—foundation, subflooring, walls, and roof—so, too, the storyboard process starts with the "concept," or the problem to be solved, and moves along in a creative interplay of ideas and suggestions until the desired solution has taken shape.

And that is exactly what happened in the session with the utility after only two hours of storyboarding. The once-skeptical executives were astounded. One of them admitted to us afterwards that the group initially thought storyboarding was, in his words, "a real Mickey Mouse technique." They couldn't imagine that it could be of benefit in their situation. But more progress was made in two hours of storyboarding than the group had made in the previous two years of endless meetings and unproductive wrangling. Everyone agreed that the storyboarding technique had crystallized the overall concept of what management wanted to achieve, clarified the necessary action steps, and defined the progression of tasks.

Many people wonder how something so simple can possibly work to unravel complex questions. After all, a five-year-old can be taught to put cards up on the wall. Yet to paraphrase a line of poetry, simplicity is elegance, and it usually takes just one session to convince people of the richness of the storyboarding technique. The power it has to engage and stimulate people and to unleash their productivity is remarkable.

We believe that the high level of participation demanded by storyboarding is one reason that it works so well. Instead of the typical meeting situation in which the troops are forced to endure endless and often garbled rhetoric, in a storyboard situation the facilitator engages all people in a focused discussion.

This approach also heightens the concentration of individual group members as they become immersed in the problem at hand. Participants begin to embellish and expand on one another's ideas, unlike what often happens in brainstorming when rather than adding to the proposed idea, half the people in the group are busy marshaling their thoughts to rebut it. "That's not going to work," they think, or "My department will never buy that."

In addition, the initial anonymity (people don't have to sign their names to their idea cards) encourages free expression and critical thinking. The value of anonymity was brought home to us in a focus group we conducted for Illinois Power. That group, comprised of folks from the community, was set up to help the Illinois Power economic development team become more effective.

Originally scheduled to run from 8:00 A.M. until noon, the session was conducted just like a conventional focus group, with people brainstorming and putting things on flip charts around the room. When we realized after two hours that no new ideas were emerging, we assumed that everyone had said everything they wanted to say. To our surprise, however, several of the team members pressed us to try the storyboarding technique that we had previously described to them. So instead of ending the meeting early, we spent the remaining two hours doing a storyboard process. The result: At least three significant new ideas emerged concerning ways in which the development team could better serve the community.

As it turned out, some of the focus group participants had been reluctant to verbalize their ideas in front of the group. In our experience, that is often the case. Many people are simply frightened by the thought of speaking their minds in public. But stimulated by the discussion and given the chance to express themselves anonymously, they too can provide valuable input.

Storyboarding, then, can be an inestimable tool for getting to the heart of customer problems, and innovative response to customer problems is the stuff of business legend.

SOLVING THE COMMUNICATIONS DILEMMA

Intracompany communication is a hot topic these days. People fret about it in management meetings, employees complain about it around the water cooler, and everyone agrees on the need for more and better dialogue. But several questions remain: Is anyone really communicating? How many organizations have a formal plan to facilitate better communication?

One of our clients, Whirlpool, understands better than most the importance of formalizing communications. At its Lavergne, Tennessee, manufacturing plant, the company has developed an entire center devoted solely to increasing the level of interaction between management and production employees. The center, which is actually located on the manufacturing floor, contains several museum-quality display booths that disseminate division and union news, highlight corporate initiatives, and answer employee questions using storyboarding techniques. In addition, people on the plant floor have direct access to a communications manager.

More important, the center is part of a much broader communications plan that encourages face-to-face interaction between management and production people, proposes electronic communication technology, oversees written communication, and holds managers accountable for communications in their performance process.

A formal plan is important because not everyone responds to the various forms of communication in the same way. Some people like it written, some want information delivered face-to-face, and some don't care about the method, but they do care about the quality and the frequency. Obviously, meeting the needs of a diverse work group requires experimentation with various options—quarterly town hall–type meetings perhaps, or skip-level meetings that allow top management to hear from people once or twice removed from the usual information chain, or implementation of a 360-degree feedback approach. The point is that management can't depend on a haphazard communication system. It must consider the various styles and needs of its work group audience and then devise a formal plan for delivering information.

Storyboarding is an ideal way to share ideas and concepts, throwing them into the public arena for discussion and tapping a team's collective creativity to figure out where and how an idea might work in any given function or department within a company. The technique helps break through interdepartmental barriers because it promotes face-to-face communication and a lively give-and-take among diverse personalities focused on a common goal.

Working with various client teams, we have repeatedly noticed that storyboarding enhances a team's cohesiveness. The interplay of meaningful communication has a way of binding people together. This is especially true of cross-functional teams, like those we set up at Whirlpool and at Bristol-Myers Squibb.

Members of a cross-functional team are often near-strangers to one another. That's because they work in different departments and receive different training; even their outlook is different. But once team members participate in a story-boarding session together, employees from manufacturing or accounting or purchasing or any other department often find that they are not as far apart as they once thought. To solidify a team, we suggest that the group storyboard. That way, any ideas that come out of the team belong to the group, not to individuals.

The bonding element inherent in storyboarding worked to particularly good effect with a Whirlpool global team. The members of the team spoke several different languages and came from wildly different backgrounds—not just different job descriptions, but different countries, continents, and political situations. For example, among them was an engineer who had never been outside communist China before finding himself set down in the midwestern United States. How could such diversity be melded into one high-functioning group of men and women? Storyboards helped us overcome the hurdles.

We storyboarded national character traits and had team members decide which traits they liked and which they disliked. As it turned out, there was a high level of agreement on what people liked as well as what they didn't like. The best learning of all, they said, was the discovery that they all disliked "arrogance" in others! The storyboarding experiment helped to clarify the team concept for everyone. And that was no small accomplishment considering that many of the participants came from countries in which orders come from above and are followed without question. In such situations, the team concept is totally alien to the culture.

Storyboarding, then, can help a company improve communication and planning at all levels. What's more, establishing storyboarding as an integral part of planning brings clarity to an organization's internal workings.

At Illinois Power, for example, we suggested using storyboarding to help ease the transition to a new culture emphasizing teams. The plan to introduce teams and to increase the participation of the workforce at all levels amounted to radical and far-reaching change for the traditionally structured utility. Top management recognized that such an organizational metamorphosis would require a thorough reeducation program. Employees would have to reassess their views of the company as a whole as well as their individual roles within it. But determining how an implementation should be constructed was no easy task.

Storyboarding uncovered potential barriers to the transition, which could then be addressed in the plan. Among the items dealt with in the session were management and employee resistance, closed lines of communication, rigid and hierarchical bureaucracy, and outdated facilities. This particular storyboard ended up serving as the foundation for Illinois Power's implementation plan for the new team culture.

Getting Started with Storyboarding

Supplies
1. A meeting room with plenty of blank wall space.
2. An unbiased facilitator.
3. Pin boards and pins or drafting tape.
4. At least 10 4x6 index cards for every participant.
5. Water-soluble felt-tip markers in blue, black, and red.
6. Several different colored press-on ¾-inch dots.

Procedure
1. Facilitator asks leading questions, and group agrees on "topic card." (See Figure 10-1.)
2. Participants record their thoughts regarding the topic on index cards.
3. A facilitator gathers the "detail" cards, discusses each card with group, and clusters them by topic.
4. Once three to four detail cards are in a cluster, group determines "header card" that describes the cluster. Header card is then printed in red.
5. Once all cards are discussed and headers created, facilitator determines the number of "priority dots" to be given to each participant. Priority dots identify most significant headers and most significant detail cards.
6. Storyboard is either left on the wall for group reference or typed and distributed to all members.

Guidelines
1. Facilitator prepares leading questions beforehand.
2. Only one idea per card.
3. The more ideas the better.
4. No criticism of any idea.

Criteria for Good Questions
1. Induce curiosity.
2. Encourage positive thinking.
3. Strive for consensus.
4. Prevent termination of discussion.

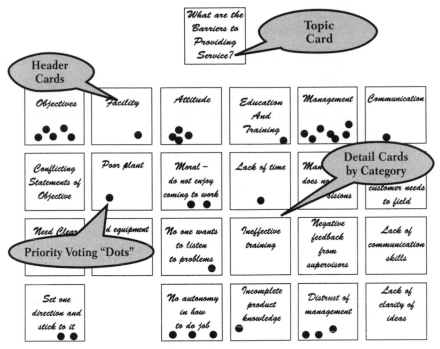

FIGURE 10-1. Storyboard example.

Facilitator's Role
1. Create pleasant, informal atmosphere.
2. Lead discussion to mobilize group's creative energy and resolve conflicts.
3. Question conclusions or answers in noncompetitive, nonhierarchical way.
4. Provide positive feedback.
5. Keep process moving.
6. Stimulate group to work on its own.

Things to Keep in Mind During Session
1. What has been achieved so far?
2. Where do we stand?
3. What still needs to be done?

STORYBOARDING: THE PROCESS

As consultants, we have seen every imaginable variety of story-board technique, some using nothing more complicated than a bunch of index cards and a fistful of markers, others utilizing charts, pictures, drawings or computer-generated printouts, and some dependent on information technology networks.

While electronic storyboarding is fine for collecting ideas and even for some degree of brainstorming, it cannot generate the creative energy that is sparked by in-person storyboard sessions. In these sessions, you are likely to see people jumping up from their chairs to point at various pieces of the puzzle. Some may even move a card from one place on the storyboard to another in order to prove that a particular idea fits better elsewhere. The increase in spontaneity and enthusiastic communication moves the meeting along at a fast pace. And because everyone is working from the same road map, it's easier to build consensus.

From a procedural standpoint, storyboarding evolves in a logical progression as mentioned above. First, the team identifies the topic to be defined or the problem to be solved, and this is written on a card and posted at the top of the story-board. Then it establishes a "purpose," meaning the reasons for pursuing the topic. The facilitator allows the participants time to sit and answer the question or problem, jotting down their thoughts, one idea per card. The facilitator then collects the cards as participants continue to write more thoughts and may choose to sort the cards moving duplications to the back of the stack. When the group has completed the writing exercise, the facilitator reads each card aloud, invites discussion, and asks the participants to suggest how the cards might be clustered or positioned on the wall. As the discussion proceeds, all miscellaneous ideas that don't seem to fit anywhere else are held onto and placed in one section of the board. Nothing is discarded, no matter how useless it might seem, because you never know when the idea offered at 10 a.m. will prove to be the perfect piece for solving the puzzle at 2 p.m.

There are four main types of storyboards:

1. The idea board, which is used to develop a concept.
2. The planning board, which is an outline of the steps required to reach the desired result.
3. The organization board, which determines who will be responsible for what.
4. The communications board (highly visible as the process or project is carried out), allows a person or group to organize and communicate daily activities to those who need to know.

Regardless of what storyboarding is being used for, one thing remains constant—its role in nurturing creative and critical thinking.

When it comes to the mechanics of storyboarding, people often ask the practical question, "How much space do we need to adequately storyboard?" There is no cut-and-dried answer because it depends on how many people will be present at a meeting. Two people can storyboard very satisfactorily in a small office for the purpose of visualizing their ideas or mapping out potential solutions to a problem. In our experience, groups of more than 25 often suffer from the old mindset of the typical classroom where the teacher speaks and the students are silent. This type of rigor mortis kills the intended participation of storyboarding.

Every storyboarding session needs a facilitator, whose job it is to bring everyone into the discussion with stimulating questions. The facilitator should, as much as possible, let the participants run the meeting while still maintaining control and not letting the discussion get out of hand.

Criticism should be avoided, no matter how off-the-wall the suggestions might seem. An informal atmosphere and encouraging words will produce the greatest number of ideas. To that end, the facilitator strives to promote positive thinking and to create a consensus, although he or she must be careful not to terminate a discussion. Ideas must flow freely to their logical conclusions.

An American architect once mused that there are very few inferior people in the world, but lots of inferior environments. "Try to enrich your environment," he advised.[33] Storyboarding is a tool that can enrich the environment of any organization, no matter the specific needs. Storyboarding can be adapted to fit so that anyone can capture the magic.

Having examined planning and problem solving, we turn our attention in the next chapter to the third element of successful execution the Disney way. As Walt knew so well, grand ideas are nothing without proper emphasis on the details.

Questions to Ask
- Do you formalize communications through the utilization of storyboards?
- Do teams of all sizes use storyboarding as a way to visualize their barriers, goals, problems, solutions, and project plans?
- Do you promote the use of storyboarding in meetings involving sensitive topics?
- Do you offer assistance in storyboard facilitation to teams in need?
- Do all employees know how to conduct a storyboarding session and in which situations this technique is particularly useful?
- Do you invite your customers and suppliers to participate in storyboarding sessions to gain their feedback and assistance in planning and problem solving?

Actions to Take
- Train all employees in the technique of storyboarding.
- Provide teams with areas to storyboard and the flexibility to leave them visible for as long as needed.
- Use storyboarding in planning sessions to develop timelines and project assignments; use the storyboard as a dynamic tool which can be changed, revised, and updated as needed.

- Use storyboarding to gain anonymous input from all meeting participants, particularly when there are sensitive topics at hand.
- Develop a formal communication plan that defines who, what, when, and how communications are made to all employees. Schedule storyboard sessions with all employees to gather ideas for improvement.

THE MIGHTY MARKER

Storyboarding was used throughout the two-year life of the Whirlpool Global No-Frost team. Everyone participated. We kept cards and markers on hand, and we would hand them out whenever scheduling or other questions arose. The cards were particularly effective with cross-functional teams as people's different functions seemed to encourage participation. According to Jerry, "A bunch of engineers in a room will produce few cards, but when they are joined by manufacturing, purchasing, and marketing, diverse points of view come up on the boards, and discussion can become extremely lively, heated, and finally productive."

Storyboarding, Jerry found, was a valuable way to get ideas and reactions out of team members. If a deadline was under discussion, he didn't want the team members sitting back and saying silently to themselves, "This will never be." He told them he wanted everybody's opinions on the cards because only when the barriers are spelled out is it possible to overcome them. "They don't want to stand up and talk about their doubts, so storyboarding is a way for people to get their thoughts on cards anonymously. It's a tremendously helpful technique for seeing a way of eliminating barriers." It was also a way for the team to reach a consensus and to figure out exactly where each subteam stood within the overall schedule.

GIVE DETAILS
TOP BILLING

There are two words that make [operations] work around here...quality and pride. If you design, build, operate, and maintain with quality, people will take pride in what they do.[34]

DICK NUNIS

Chairman, Walt Disney Attractions

B usiness people of every stripe place a great deal of importance on seeing the "big picture" or coming up with the grand idea. But seldom understood is the fact that details give the big picture depth; they bring the grand idea clearly into focus and produce pride in workmanship. Paying attention to the little things is what turns the vision into a top-quality product or an outstanding service. As the great architect Mies van der Rohe once put it, "God is in the details."[35]

No one had to tell Walt Disney the significance that seeming trifles can have when excellence is the goal. Perhaps because he possessed an artist's eye, he recognized that attention to detail was the key to complete realization of his dreams. As a result, the company he founded has no equal when it comes to creating the thousands of intricate drawings needed to produce nonpareil animation, bring together the mind-boggling number of parts required to build a Disneyland or a Disney World, or carefully attend to the numerous small details that make every guest's experience a magical one.

Often overlooked in Disney's awe-inspiring success is how the company as an organization has managed to give extravagant attention to detail without bankrupting itself. It has achieved a careful balance between the competing demands of the bottom line and the quest for perfection. The key to this balancing act is contained in the Disney philosophy that everyone—from the groundskeepers at the parks and the animators in the movie studio to the number crunchers in the accounting department—is responsible for doing whatever it takes to deliver the "good show." Even Michael Eisner has "trash collecting" in his job description when he's visiting one of the theme parks! When all parties are convinced of the importance of their individual roles, nothing will be left to chance.

Most of the companies we work with are far removed from the Disney environment of entertainment, yet they too have recognized that obsessive attention to detail can pay huge dividends. Thus, they are calling on "casts" of employees to present their own version of the good show to an "audience" comprised of suppliers and customers, and in doing so, these companies are consistently delivering quality products and services to their target markets.

A RELENTLESS SEARCH FOR PERFECTION

There is a photograph in the Disney archives of Walt and ten of his animators standing around a studio table. In the middle of the table are five live penguins. The birds are all turned toward Walt Disney as if they know where their next meal is coming from. This arresting and charming image perfectly captures so much of the Disney ethos and magic—the element of surprise, the embrace of the animal kingdom, and always, the relentless search for perfection.

Disney, who was determined to exceed customers' expectations, was dissatisfied with the movements of his animated movie animals. They were good, but they weren't perfect. Up until that time, his animators had relied on photographic stills or movie clips to give them the models for their figures. It was clear to Walt that the animators could do better if they were able to copy the real thing—ergo, the penguins.

"How can we do better?" is the question Walt Disney asked at every turn. But then complacency is unnatural to the perfectionist. He strove continually to improve the quality of his products. "Whenever I ride an attraction," he once said, "I'm thinking of what's wrong with the thing and asking myself how can it be improved."[36]

The story is told that after Disneyland was already up and running, the boss stopped in to take a ride on the Jungle Cruise attraction. He emerged furious. The ride was advertised as taking seven minutes, but he had timed it at only four-and-a-half minutes. The very idea that a guest might be short-changed was antithetical to the Disney culture and to Walt's vision of quality; he ordered the ride lengthened immediately. Moreover, he made it clear that carelessness toward details would not be tolerated, for such an attitude might cause guests to start doubting Disney's trustworthiness, the heart and soul of his management philosophy and personal credo.

Meticulous attention to detail is also characteristic of the Disney animated films. In *Snow White*, for example, viewers don't see drops of water just dripping from a bar of soap, in itself an unusual level of detail in animated films. Instead, they see glistening bubbles that actually twinkle in the candlelight.

Creating such film magic required a staff of skilled animators, of course, and here, too, Walt refused to leave anything to chance. To make sure that he would always have a sufficient number of talented artists to meet his demanding standards, Walt began in-house training courses and eventually made a deal that brought teachers from an art school to work with his animators.

In fact, no corner of the organization escaped Walt's obsession with perfection. Thoroughly convinced that no detail was too small to be ignored in order to provide his guests with an exceptional experience, the boss made his touch everywhere apparent. He determined that garbage cans should be spaced exactly 25 feet apart all around Disneyland. He ordered that the highest-quality paint be used on rides and buildings, going so far as to specify that real gold or silver be used for any gilding or silvering. He even hired someone whose job it was to patrol Disneyland twice a month to make certain that all the colors in the park were in harmony!

The master entertainer instinctively knew that the whole package—colors, sounds, smells—had an impact on how guests received the show.

If this holistic, integrated approach to entertainment seems excessive, one need only think of a promising restaurant experience that went awry because of one disagreeable factor. Perhaps the food was first-class, the service pleasant, and the decor attractive, but the background music assailed a diner's ears and made it impossible to enjoy the meal. One jarring element can undermine a host of favorable impressions in a restaurant or anywhere else, and Walt Disney wasn't about to risk such a misstep.

That's why street cleaners at Disney World are given extra training at Disney University to ensure that they respond in a positive and helpful fashion to questions from departing guests. It might seem strange to train street cleaners in customer service, but the company learned a few years back that these employees receive the greatest number of unstructured questions from park guests. An exhausted couple with three hungry children in tow might ask where they can get a quick, inexpensive dinner, for instance. To make sure that a guest's last impression after a wonderful day in the park isn't ruined by a don't-ask-me-it's-not-my-job attitude, the Disney organization decrees an extra three days of interpersonal skills training for the clean-up crew. They take a proactive approach to head off potentially damaging situations. The Disney organization realizes that the entire "whole show" is critical; the way the street cleaner treats the guest is as important or even more important than the way the guest is treated on Space Mountain.

MAINTAINING A DELICATE BALANCE

When it came to pursuing the often elusive ideal of perfection, Walt Disney spared no expense. The previously mentioned reworking of the Jiminy Cricket character in *Pinocchio,* after the costly animation process was already well under way, is but one example. When it was discovered that a merry-go-round at Disney World was installed two inches off center, the company insisted that it be moved. Who would notice? you might wonder. The Disney folks not only noticed, but they reasoned that if the carousel were not set right, thousands of guests would take home vacation pictures that provided an imperfect memory of their visit to the park.

You see, the Kodak Company estimates that 5 percent of all the photographs taken in North America are taken at the Disney theme parks, and many of those taken in Disney World are from an angle that includes the merry-go-round in the background. An off-center merry-go-round would make those pictures look strange, because the merry-go-round appears centered as one passes through the castle. The company decided, naturally, that the imperfect merry-go-round had to be moved, despite the hefty expense involved.

But we must make clear that "sparing no expense" has never meant profligate spending. Walt Disney was always well aware of the bottom line, and he expected that the money spent would be returned in customer satisfaction and employee loyalty. The way Walt saw it, meticulous attention to detail provided a level of quality that cast members could take pride in, and he knew that when workers are proud of their product, it is reflected in the kind of service they give to customers.

But when it came to spending on items unrelated to providing the good show, the boss was actually known as something of a penny-pincher. He never built a splendidly pompous, ego-enhancing headquarters building, nor did he ever spend a nickel on advertising his theme park. Disney reasoned that his television shows provided advertising aplenty, so why waste money paying for it? In today's environment Disney has a large advertising budget but still does not waste money on backstage areas.

Walt also kept a sharp eye on financial arrangements and partnerships, not hesitating to protect his own interests. Although a licensing deal in the early 1930s brought in

$300,000 the first year—with Walt's share providing half of the company's annual profits that year—he quickly discovered a major drawback. The deal called for his percentage of the profits to increase as more items were sold, but since novelty items sold fast and then faded from the market, the licensee would make a lot more money than Disney would. Walt canceled the arrangement and set up an in-house marketing division.

Today, Disney executives ask cast members to balance what they call "quality cast experience," "quality guest experience," and "quality business practice." The product should deliver value in all three areas, pleasing cast members, customers, and corporate bean counters and balancing them as needed. The company firmly believes, as Walt did, that obsessive attention to detail in all respects is the key to delivering a sterling experience that will keep guests coming back while holding costs to a level that still maintains profit margins.

In our experience, successful companies like Disney balance business and creative needs by insisting on strict adherence to a set of core values, emphasizing the importance of details in exceeding customer expectations, and encouraging innovation and risk taking within a specified set of boundaries. Disney makes no bones about its belief that creativity works best within a specified framework. In a 1996 interview with *Fortune* magazine, Peter Schneider, president of the Animation Division, called deadlines "a key ingredient to creativity."[37] They force people to focus on the project at hand, to produce *something*—good, bad, or indifferent—that will at least serve to spark the next idea, he said. And, of course, deadlines also keep costs from spiraling out of control.

Many of the companies we advise have devised winning strategies that similarly balance top-of-the-line quality with innovation and bottom-line performance.

John Dunn's hotel properties consistently rank at the top in opinion polls because of his insistence on quality and attention to detail. Employees end up caring for the properties as much as they care for their own homes, picking up trash dropped on the floor, straightening a lampshade as they pass by, and tidying newspapers left scattered about the lobby.

Everyone from the desk clerk to the banquet manager is trained to react rather than overlook.

One of Dunn's managers insists that every item on the breakfast bar—coffee, juice, rolls, butter—be placed in exactly the same place every day. Now you might ask what difference it makes if the coffee pot is on the left or the right. But the manager recognizes that repeat guests, and particularly the targeted business traveler, will appreciate not having to hunt for the decaffeinated coffee or figure out which is the apple juice and which is the orange.

At BellSouth, attention to details means that when an installation and maintenance crew is at a particular location, members know to make the appropriate preventive repairs that will head off future problems and save another time-consuming, money-devouring visit at a later date. Just as with the Dunn hotel employees, being proactive is an important ingredient in balancing quality and costs.

MEASURING FOR SUCCESS

Paying attention to detail also means measuring results. This concept seems almost too rudimentary to mention, but experience has taught us that many organizations make little or no effort to assess results, either in terms of operating objectives or in terms of performance standards and customer satisfaction.

In our Dream Retreats, for example, we frequently ask participants, "How many of you feel that you would be more successful if you made fewer mistakes and produced your product more quickly?" Everyone always raises a hand. But seldom does even one hand stay in the air when we follow up with, "How many of you are making quality and time measurements for your key business processes?"

We can't emphasize strongly enough the importance of implementing some system for gauging quality level, process time, customer satisfaction, and product cost, as well as negative elements such as errors of judgment and process mistakes. All too often, companies give little thought to measuring processes in their entirety, even though doing so need not be a complicated task. But without measurements, an organization cannot possibly know which processes are working efficiently and effectively, what products and services are meeting quality standards, and whether or not customer requirements are being satisfied.

Identifying processes and mapping the functions involved is key to increasing efficiency. In many organizations, however, processes seem to be hit-or-miss affairs, the result of haphazard growth. When a team takes the time to map the details of a process, the results are usually an eye-opener. "Why would anyone design a process like that?" baffled executives ask. No one did design it, of course, and that's just the problem. The process simply mushroomed in all directions as well-meaning managers added a step here and required a memo there. Before long, what once was a relatively smooth-functioning process has turned into a Hydra-headed monster.

Dr. William Cross, the vice president with whom we worked at Mead Johnson and whom we first mention in Chapter 4, found this out when teams in his department decided to take a look at certain key business processes. They uncovered many redundant and non-value-added elements that had been built into the system over the course of several years. Dr. Cross was astounded to discover that mapping a single work process related to releasing a new product produced a "flow chart that when it was all put together end to end, was about seven feet high and about two and a half feet wide, and was in very small print. So it was extremely complex."[38]

By mapping out the details of the complex process, however, the team was able to determine which steps could safely be discontinued. The new streamlined process reduced the usual cycle time for a product release by about two weeks.

Something similar occurred when Bill Capodagli was working with the South African utilities company mentioned in Chapter 9. After every step in the procurement process had been documented, more than 100 square feet of a wall in the project planning center were covered with index cards. Needless to say, the process was hopelessly complex and very often redundant so that capital materials procurement was taking as much as a year and a half, with seven or eight months of that eaten up by the internal bureaucracy.

Astonished company executives could only wonder how it had happened that pieces of paper were going back and forth for months on end, and for absolutely no reason at all. Once the process was streamlined, the savings in time and money was considerable.

For another of our clients, Father Carl of Abbey Press, the process-mapping helped heighten his sensitivity toward the needs of team members. Recognizing that his output would become someone else's input and knowing what that person planned to do with it made Father Carl more aware of his responsibilities in the manufacturing process. "Now I give good quality output to the next person," Father Carl says, "so that he or she can add additional quality onto what has been received."[39] The end result is a much more efficient and effective manufacturing process.

When we work with a team on a quality initiative, a willingness to become immersed in details is a must. At Mead Johnson, for example, the exhaustive process began with the creation of a complaint analysis team to determine the path traveled by product complaints, either from an individual or from another company. It took us three to four months to complete the flow chart documenting each step involved. The team interviewed every department along the route, and when the flow chart was done, each department was asked to check it for accuracy.

Simultaneously, the team followed one sample complaint through the entire handling process and clocked the amount of time each step took. Multiplying the time factor by the department's charge-out rate allowed the team to assess costs. The team discovered that a single complaint traveling through the analysis system took an average of 30 days and cost the company up to $910 from beginning to end. Having established its data, the team was then able to draw up a new flow chart for an ideal system.

One change drastically reduced the number of complaints that were still being stored after the process was completed.

Before the analysis, all complaints were being held for four months, even though most of them were never looked at again. The team logically determined that only those complaints that posed a potential legal threat, packaging that had allegedly been tampered with, or those that involved a federal, state, or local government agency needed to be retained. This one simple change of process saved the company considerable time.

Not all of the team's proposals and recommendations could be instituted immediately because some depended on decisions in other divisions. But initial forecasts pointed to eventual savings of $123 per complaint. Dr. Cross said, "The teams have saved in dollars thus far tens of thousands which have already [produced] a payback."[40]

The message for management, then, is to look at your business in a holistic manner the way Disney looks at its show. Carefully examine all the details that affect the way your product or service is provided to customers. In other words, go the extra mile, or as the folks at Disney might say, "Bump the lamp."

This cryptic phrase originated when the movie *Roger Rabbit* was being made, and it relates to a scene in which someone bumps into a lamp, causing the shadow it casts to wobble. Initially, there were no shadows in the scene, which the animators immediately spotted as being unrealistic, so they went back and did the hundreds of drawings needed to bring perfection to these few seconds of the film.

"Bump the lamp" has become shorthand at Disney for management's commitment to doing things the right way, down to the tiniest detail. CEO Michael Eisner has raised the bar of performance—to "bump the lamp" and strive for excellence in all they do. We encourage you to make it the philosophy in your organization too.

Questions to Ask
- Do your cross-functional teams map all the critical details of processes in order to determine which steps can be safely eliminated?
- Do your employees and teams make quality and time measurements of their critical processes?
- Do your employees routinely ask, "How can we do this better?"

- Do you include meticulous attention to detail as part of your organization's values?

- Do you reward people in your organization for detecting inconsistencies or defects in the products you produce?

Actions to Take

- Appoint a "details squad" to get fanatical about the details which make a difference to your customers.

- Continuously evaluate the effectiveness of your processes.

- Make attention to detail a part of organizational values.

- Evaluate how "little things" can make a difference in the way you serve customers or turn out products.

- Don't assume you can wow a customer with the big picture at the expense of details.

THE POWER OF RIGHT AND LEFT

When we first began our work with the Global No-Frost team, we asked each team member to complete the Myers-Briggs Type Indicator to assess his or her personality and unique styles. We knew the team needed people who preferred detailed work as well as those who thought more conceptually.

From the outset, Jerry surrounded himself with what he calls "detail people," who made up 80 percent of the team. "I'm such a big picture person," he says of himself, "details can be my Achilles heel." The team's two engineering managers, one for manufacturing and one for technology, were both strong on details. Before they really understood Jerry's freewheeling personality, they were frustrated with his approach. They would hand him a carefully detailed exposition, running to some five or six pages, of an idea or a concept they had developed. Jerry was barely able to read the first two or three pages before his eyes glazed over. The two team members thought he didn't care. In truth, he did care, but he felt that the details were their responsibility. The same was true of the times that he discussed his own concepts with them. "Well, how would you do that?" was their response, to which Jerry replied, "I wouldn't know. That's your job."

The interesting aspect of these encounters was the reception among team members of the Myers-Briggs results. Once they understood that people process information differently, that there is no right or wrong way to do so, they became much more tolerant of each other. The two managers, for instance, learned that to get an idea past Jerry, they had to give him the essence of it. He trusted them to work out the details. Conversely, Jerry began to understand that when he wanted to share an idea or a concept with any of the detail men, he had to put some meat on it.

The team story was, in many of its aspects, the story of learning to communicate. "Nobody changes their personality," Jerry has said, "but we all tried to be more sensitive to others."

THE MAGIC CONTINUES

Well after 40 some odd years in the business, my greatest reward, I think, is I've been able to build this wonderful organization...also to have the public appreciate and accept what I've done all these years—that is a great reward.[41]

WALT DISNEY

From a young boy's doodling to a worldwide empire with a host of magical characters that are instantly recognizable by both children and adults—this is the Walt Disney Company's legend and legacy.

Would Walt recognize his brainchild as it is today? The physical plant has greatly expanded, of course. Disneyland offers a variety of new attractions. Disney World, which hadn't yet opened when Walt died, is now comprised of four separate parks, including the newest and highly celebrated Animal Kingdom. And Disneyland Paris, Tokyo Disneyland, and the South American park, still in the planning stage, illustrate the company's international reach.

Yet chances are that Walt would feel right at home. That's because the culture and traditions he established—his dreams, his beliefs, his goals, and his style of managing the business— provided the direction that makes the Walt Disney Company one of the most admired companies in the world. The "good show" mentality, which dictates pulling out all the stops to exceed guests' expectations and which demands superior

193

performance from everyone, holds as much sway now as it did when Walt Disney first decreed it.

That the Walt Disney Company manages continually to top itself and delight the world with its magic year after year, decade after decade, is a tribute to its leadership, both past and present. Part of Walt Disney's greatness was that he laid down a solid foundation of beliefs and values, including a standard of performance excellence and a mechanism (Disney University) for inculcating his cast members with these values. And part of Michael Eisner's greatness is that he recognized the value of Walt's legacy and made sure that the foundation would remain strong.

A NEW DREAM WEAVER ENTERS THE KINGDOM

After Walt's death in 1966, his brother Roy, who came out of retirement to help bring to life what was perhaps Walt's biggest dream, Disney World, continued to run the company with the same adherence to the basic values. But when Roy died in 1971, a crucial piece of the original philosophy began to disintegrate. The company no longer seemed willing to take the risks needed to maintain the vibrant Disney spirit. The company's vision appeared to shrink to an either/or view: Either we can be creative or we can protect our sound financial position. It chose the safe, conservative approach.

Essentially, the company was in a holding pattern from 1971 until 1984, when Michael Eisner came on board after a stunningly successful run at Paramount Pictures. Combining the creativity, vision, and daring of Walt with the business savvy of Roy, Eisner impressed the board of directors as the perfect figure to reawaken the spirit that had originally propelled the Walt Disney Company to greatness. The board's impressions of Eisner's genius proved to be accurate beyond anyone's imaginings.

Long an admirer of Walt Disney and a not-too-shabby dreamer in his own right—his creativity had helped to rejuvenate a then-faltering Paramount, Eisner embraced Disney's four-pillared philosophy with gusto. From the start, he recognized that a much-needed revitalization could be achieved through a vigorous return to the company's core competencies. Therefore, building a successful movie and television company became Eisner's main goal.

Cognizant of the value of Disney's bread-and-butter animation talent, he decreed that the studio would turn out at least one new animated film each year. (In the 18 years between Walt's death and Eisner's arrival, Disney had made only four new animated films.) With the help and support of a group of extremely talented executives—widely known as the Dream Team—Eisner has turned out a string of animated hits as well as successful live-action films. And in a nod to the times, not all the live-action films are designed exclusively for the family market; many appeal to diverse audiences with wide-ranging tastes.

The company's success in the world of television is equally impressive. Among the many pieces in the company's television mosaic are the Disney Channel, an interest in the ESPN sports network through its ownership of ABC, Saturday morning children's programming, and *The Wonderful World of Disney* and made-for-TV movies.

Storytelling continues to be central to the Walt Disney Company's *Dream* principle, and Eisner, who early in his career worked in television programming, certainly understands the value of a good story. So it's not surprising that the heart and soul of the Walt Disney Company is not at corporate headquarters or in one of the magical theme parks, but rather in the almost invisible corner of the kingdom that is Walt Disney Imagineering.

The 2000 Imagineers, the group whose sole purpose is to carry on the Disney creative spirit, spend their time dreaming up the ever more sophisticated thrills that are the Disney product. And despite the amazing technology the product incorporates, Bran Ferren, head of research and development at Walt Disney Imagineering, has said that the Disney power comes neither from its advanced technology nor from its immense design talent. What holds the value at Disney is, as Ferren recently expressed it to *I.D. Magazine* contributing editor John Hockenberry, "the ancient magic of storytelling."[42]

No matter the product or the audience, excellence is still a Disney goal, although Eisner readily concedes that not every offering reaches the target. He is quick to point out, however, that that's okay, because it's important that the company not become complacent, overconfident, or arrogant. Nourishing the company's principal asset, creativity, requires an atmosphere that says it's all right to fail sometimes. Otherwise, fear of ridicule will prevent people from voicing the scores of ideas that might seem weird or unworkable but that sometimes contain the seeds of brilliance.

In this, Eisner perfectly reflects the Dream principle: Give everyone license to dream, and tap the creativity those dreams embody.

COMMITTED TO BELIEFS

The spectacle, the excitement, the breadth of product—all of these things contribute to the legend. Yet if there is one thing that keeps people coming back, it is the consistency of the experience. The Walt Disney Company is the master at creating controlled environments that never disappoint. Because the company goes to great lengths to communicate its beliefs and traditions to every cast member, the Disney product offers people a comforting familiarity that is hard to duplicate in today's fast-paced world. That's not to say that there are no surprises, merely that all the surprises are on the upside.

Disney's insistence that customers be treated like guests continues to be of paramount importance in providing that always-positive, expectation-exceeding experience. Thus a visitor to any of the theme parks will find that a question is answered as pleasantly today as it would have been in the Disneyland of the 1950s and 1960s. Cast members are never too busy to stop and chat with guests, crowd control is performed with a smile, and lost children are pampered with small pleasures. The human touch is still very much in evidence.

Yet without a corresponding belief in and commitment to employees, the customer philosophy would soon founder. The two go together, as the song says, like a horse and carriage, and you can't have one without the other.

Maintaining the company's focus amid enormous growth—the number of employees has more than tripled since Eisner took over in 1984—requires that Disney be ever more vigilant about recognizing the significant role that each cast member plays and then emphasizing that all the pieces are needed to ensure the success of the entire team. By making cast members feel that their input makes a difference, Disney inspires further contributions.

Not to be overlooked is the company's unwavering belief in the power of partnering. Walt Disney never shied from teaming up with a variety of partners to achieve his goals, and the same holds true for Eisner. The long list of profitable ventures includes a five-film deal with Pixar Animation Studios, the Steve Jobs computer-animation company with whom Disney made the Academy Award-winning *Toy Story* in 1995, and an arrangement concluded in the spring of 1998 that made PepsiCo the exclusive beverage supplier at Disney's regional entertainment centers. In addition, Disney and McDonald's continue to strengthen their strategic alliance with the addition of more promotional tie-ins.

Honesty, reliability, loyalty, and respect for the individual are as much a part of the Disney culture today as they were in Walt's day. And the way the company sees it, living those beliefs still means working hard to exceed a guest's expectations and always delivering the good show. What's more, if customers are the reason for being, it naturally follows that *everyone*—cast members, partners, suppliers, and so on—must be united in their effort to reach the goal. This is the *Believe* principle in action.

THRIVING ON CHALLENGE

Michael Eisner would never be described as a gambler, but calculated risk taking is another matter entirely. His move to

Disney was in itself something of a calculated risk. His great success at Paramount gave him virtually his pick of jobs, but he chose to cast his lot with a company that had stumbled badly after the death of its legendary founder. Many people wondered if anyone could ever fill Walt's shoes. Neither hubris nor naïveté prompted Eisner to accept the challenge; rather, his conviction that his abilities fit well with the company's traditions induced him to take the job.

If saying yes to the job was Eisner's first risky move at Disney, it certainly was not his last. One of his initial decisions involved approval of the script for the decidedly un-Disneylike *Down and Out in Beverly Hills,* an R-rated film far removed from the studio's typical family-oriented offerings. The studio had already begun to move gingerly away from its traditional fare before Eisner arrived, but with the exception of *Splash,* no movie produced by the previous management had been a hit. Eisner's early success with *Down and Out, Ruthless People,* and a series of other film releases proved that like Walt, he has uncanny instincts for what audiences want.

One of Eisner's most daring moves in recent years, and one that left both critics and competitors sputtering, was the 1996 acquisition of Capital Cities/ABC for $18.9 billion. The marriage, which cemented a relationship that began when ABC helped Walt Disney open Disneyland in 1955, silenced critics who had questioned whether Eisner had the nerve to make a really big acquisition.

In another gutsy move, Eisner chose to renovate a seedy theater in New York's bawdy Times Square area and to bring *The Lion King* to Broadway. At the time the commitment was made, no one could say for sure that a neighborhood known for its sex shops and drug trafficking could be successfully transformed.

More recently, Eisner made another bold departure from Disney tradition by sinking $800 million into the Animal Kingdom, which opened in April 1998. "It's basically antiDisney," Joe Rohde, the Imagineer in charge of the park, said in an *I.D. Magazine* interview.[43] Not only does the 540-acre park feature live animals instead of the much more easily controlled animated ones but it also strips away illusion in a fashion totally uncharacteristic of Disney.

That's not to say, however, that there is *no* illusion. Disney is still in the business of creating magic, and the artfully crafted African savanna created out of Florida scrub has its quotient of illusion. But the very nature of a venue populated by 1000 wild animals means that the experience can't be tightly scripted in typical Disney style. If opening reviews are any measure, however, this daring new mix of reality and entertainment is apt to meet with typical Disney success.

A willingness to take calculated risks on innovative ideas means nothing if a company doesn't have what it takes to follow through in the execution of those ideas. With Eisner at the helm, Disney has maintained its founder's firm belief that execution requires extensive training, planning, communicating, and paying attention to detail.

The renowned Disney training program still turns out cast members who are thoroughly prepared for their roles. So successful is the program, in fact, that Disney now markets its methods to other organizations. And if planning and attention to detail are wanted, one need only look at the eight years of planning and $800 million worth of attention to detail that went into the Animal Kingdom—details so convincing that the South African ambassador to the United States was quoted in *Time* magazine as saying, "This is the bush veldt. This is my home."[44]

But perhaps nothing so thoroughly evidences the current strength of Disney's execution as its unrivaled talent for synergy. As an analyst once told Kathryn Harris of the *Los Angeles Times*, "This is a great company in an operating sense....They've gotten everything out of the mouse but the squeak."[45]

Thus, a new film begets an absolute deluge of new marketing possibilities, from domestic and international home videos and network and foreign television runs to pay-per-view and cable offerings.

And that's just the beginning. Next comes new theme park rides and characters, new products in Disney stores (toys, clothing, books, games, records, CD-ROMs), new television spinoffs, and programming ideas for Disney's radio networks. Animated features become live-action films—like *101 Dalmatians*—or Broadway stage shows such as *The Lion King* and *Beauty and the Beast*.

Once the company decides to pursue a new idea, it immediately communicates that information to every segment of the company that might be able to exploit it in every other potential market or product. This notion of cross-pollination has become a major driver of the company's profitability.

IN TUNE WITH THE NATION

Like Walt Disney himself, Michael Eisner thrives on the business of making magic. And also like Disney, he is a hands-on leader who is creating his own company lore with his attention to detail. He passes judgment on animation ideas, selects carpet for new hotels, and gives the go-ahead on TV commercials. Disguised in dark glasses and wearing a baseball cap turned back to front, he has been known to visit Disney stores to check out the merchandise and the store's appearance. His love of children's programming and his willingness to become a symbol of the company contribute to the perception that Eisner may be "more Walt than Walt."

Success of the magnitude Disney has achieved always brings out the critics and the fear-mongers, those who cry that the company is too powerful and wields too much influence in our society. But investors don't share the angst; they have driven the price of the company's stock to ever-higher highs as the century winds to a close. They sense that the Walt Disney Company has its finger firmly on the pulse of the nation, indeed the world.

There may be some disagreement as to whether the public's blood is pumping with longing for a return to the old-fashioned values of family, hard work, and excellence that Disney symbolizes, or whether a public preference for escapism is at the heart of Disney's popularity. (No one, by the way, disputes that the escapes Disney constructs are anything short of magnificent.) In any event, the crowds that flock to virtually every Disney venue would seem to bear out the assessment that Disney surely has the Midas touch, whatever its source.

Walt Disney's legacy, then, flourishes at the astonishing institution called The Walt Disney Company. Like our nation, it is a restless enterprise, always seeking new and better ways to entertain its audiences, to put on the good show. With two new theme parks under construction (Tokyo DisneySea and Disney's California Adventure), with Disney products delighting people of all nationalities in every corner of the globe, and with a giant mid-decade step into cyberspace via Disney's family-oriented Web site, Michael Eisner and his team have fearlessly catapulted Walt's company into the twenty-first century.

What's more, every dream continues to be achieved with a management style that remains true to Disney's original vision: a firm belief in core values backed up by hard work from a well-trained and dedicated team that relentlessly strives for perfection. The company today is a vital, living monument to the enduring power of Walt's way.

We have examined the ten principles that make up the Disney management style in separate chapters for the sake of our book's organization, but it is their integration and interplay that work to change companies. As you envision their implementation in your company, think in terms of a holistic integration and imagine the benefits to be derived.

For example, giving employees a chance to dream and to express their creativity not only enhances their satisfaction and encourages commitment to the company, it also opens up a vast new source of knowledge and innovative ideas from which the company can draw. By the same token, when management instills a set of firm beliefs, it doesn't just bring consistency to its operations, it encourages all parties— coworkers, partners, suppliers—to work cooperatively to further those beliefs.

Unshakable convictions, in turn, nourish the self-assurance and confidence in one's instincts that are needed to overcome a fear of risk taking. Daring to take risks encourages still further creativity and maintains the vibrancy of an organization. It creates a sense of fun and adventure that inspires individuals and teams to reach higher and work harder. And in the end, the principles that make it possible to follow through and turn the dreams into reality, that is, training, planning, communicating, and attention to detail, all double back to promote more creativity, more concern for customers, and more commitment to teamwork.

We see the cycle as one that constantly reinforces itself, and we believe that by incorporating the basic elements of the Disney management technique, every organization can lift itself out of the ranks of the ordinary. Figure E-1 shows it all in simple graphic form. Ask the questions and take the actions as outlined in these chapters. Make dreaming, believing, daring, and doing the keys to your business success.

THREE BIG WINS

Team rewards are an essential component of all good teamwork. As we mentioned earlier, we had spontaneous celebrations and we had official parties. Along the way, Jerry McColgin often took members out for a game of golf after the completion of an especially grueling project. But the big award was, of course, the year-end bonus, and herein lay a problem—how to calculate a fair bonus for an international team whose members were usually paid under a variety of bonus structures. With the help of the company COO, Jerry finally worked out a solution for the first year's bonus. But when the final bonus was to be paid, there was such a generally critical and unpleasant attitude among other members of management in the company that Jerry felt he should offer to forgo his own bonus not only to preserve others' rewards but to maintain team morale and focus. In the end, it all worked out, and Jerry received his bonus too, but we have always felt that Jerry's offer was proof of his commitment to the team.

"One of the things we encouraged from the beginning," Jerry recounts, "was to celebrate failure. I'll never forget the first time someone said that his subteam had failed in a design task. My response was to say, 'It's great to discover this now and not once

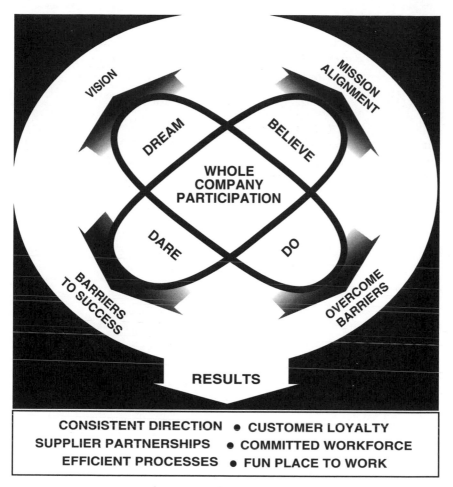

FIGURE E-1.   Dream, Believe, Dare, Do process.

we're in production.'" This was part of Jerry's way of building trust so that people were as open with their failures as with their successes.

For Jerry, looking back after the team's work was finished, this project was the best job experience he had ever had. "I looked out on the horizon and asked, 'How can I top this?'" What Jerry learned, though, is that there is no recipe. There are no hard and fast rules for a successful team project. Each team is different in its makeup, in its goals, and in its leader. If you change all the ingredients, you can't use the same recipe. Putting people first is essential. The deliverables will follow if the team is cohesive and dedicated to the goals. In the case of the Global No-Frost team, it was ten months before a pervasive sense of unity took hold, so patience is required. The team, with its diverse staff, its time pressures, and financial limits, ended its project with a memorable triumph.

"We came in ahead of schedule, under budget on investment, and with a lower product cost than promised," Jerry recounts with justifiable pride. The achievements of the team were, indeed, astounding.

NOTES

1. Bob Thomas. *Walt Disney: An American Original,* New York, Pocket Books, 1976, p. 86.
2. Joe McGowan, Peter Schneider, and Joyce E. Davis. "How Disney Keeps Ideas Coming," *Fortune,* April 1, 1996.
3. *Walt Disney's Famous Quotes,* The Walt Disney Company, 1994, p. 43.
4. Mike Vance. "Managing by Values," *Creative Thinking* (audiotape series), Chicago, Nightingale Conant Corporation.
5. "The Quiet American," *The Economist,* November 8, 1997, p. 76.
6. Van Arsdale France. *Window on Main Street: 35 Years of Creating Happiness at Disneyland Park,* Nashua, NH, Laugher Publications, Inc./Stabur Press, Inc., 1991, p. 83.
7. Van Arsdale France. *Window on Main Street: 35 Years of Creating Happiness at Disneyland Park,* Nashua, NH, Laugher Publications, Inc./Stabur Press Inc., 1991, p. 83.
8. *People Management,* Walt Disney World Company Seminar Productions, Lake Buena Vista, Florida, 1986.
9. *Walt Disney's Famous Quotes,* The Walt Disney Company, 1994, p. 9.
10. *Walt Disney's Famous Quotes,* The Walt Disney Company, 1994, p. 88.
11. *Walt Disney's Famous Quotes,* The Walt Disney Company, 1994, p. 90.
12. Thomas J. Allen. *Managing the Flow of Technology,* Cambridge, MA, The MIT Press, 1977, pp. 234–265.
13. "Time Based Competiton" (video with workbook), Harvard Business School Management Programs, 1993, p. 8.
14. Alfie Kohn. *No Contest: The Case Against Competition,* Boston, Houghton Mifflin, 1992, p. 47.
15. Alfie Kohn. *No Contest: The Case Against Competition,* Boston, Houghton Mifflin, 1992, pp. 47–48.
16. Kenneth Shouler. "King of the Garden," *Home Cigar Aficionado,* 1998, p. 5.
17. Dr. William Cross. "Changing Management Styles," WNIN—TV appearance, Evansville, Indiana, August 1993.
18. *Customer Service Track Team Report,* Bristol-Myers Squibb—Mead Johnson Nutritional Division, 1994.
19. Alex Tayor, III and Joyce E. Davis, "Iacocca's Minivan," *Fortune,* May 30, 1994.
20. Michael D. Eisner. "Letter to Shareholders," *The Walt Disney Company Annual Report,* 1997.

21. *The Walt Disney Company Annual Report,* 1996 and 1997.

22. Walt Disney. *People Management,* Walt Disney World Company Seminar Productions, Lake Buena Vista, Florida, 1986.

23. *People Management,* Walt Disney World Company Seminar Productions, Lake Buena Vista, Florida, 1986.

24. Robert Stallings. Interview with Bill Capodagli, Evansville, Indiana, 1991.

25. Special Conference Report: National Catholic Development Conference, "Offer Donors a Chance for Greatness," *Fund-Raising Management,* November 1992, p. 20.

26. Viktor Frankl. *Man's Search for Meaning,* New York, Simon and Schuster, Touchstone Books, 1984, p. 75.

27. Mary Walton. *The Deming Management Method,* New York, The Putnam Publishing Group, 1986, p. 195.

28. C. S. Hall and G. Lindzey. *Theories of Personality,* 3d ed., New York, John Wiley and Sons, 1978, p. 64.

29. Valerie Oberle. *The Disney Approach to Quality Service,* Walt Disney World Company Seminar Productions, Lake Buena Vista, Florida, November 1995.

30. Walt Disney. Carousel of Progress Attraction Video, 1964.

31. *Foundations of Leadership,* Walt Disney World Company Seminar Productions, Lake Buena Vista, Florida, October 13, 1996.

32. Disney Imagineers. *Walt Disney Imagineering: A Behind the Dreams Look at Making the Magic Real,* New York, Hyperion, 1996, p. 51.

33. David Hardy. "Think Out of the Box," *Personnel Psychology,* Winter 1996, pp. 1036–1039.

34. Dick Nonis. *The Disney Approach to Quality Service,* Walt Disney World Company Seminar Productions, Lake Buena Vista, Florida, November 1995.

35. E. J. Dionne, Jr. "Chattering Class," *The Washington Post Magazine,* December 29, 1996, p. W2.

36. *Walt Disney's Famous Quotes,* The Walt Disney Company, 1994, p. 33.

37. Joe McGowan, Peter Schneider, and Joyce E. Davis, "How Disney Keeps Ideas Coming," *Fortune,* April 1, 1996.

38. Dr. William Cross. "Changing Management Styles," WNIN—TV appearance, Evansville, Indiana, August 1993.

39. Father Carl Dietchman. "Changing Management Styles," WNIN—TV appearance, Evansville, Indiana, August 1993.

40. Dr. William Cross. "Changing Management Styles," WNIN—TV appearance, Evansville, Indiana, August 1993.

41. Russell Schroeder (ed.). *Walt Disney, His Life in Pictures,* New York, Disney Press, 1996, p. 63.

42. John Hockenberry. *I.D. Magazine*, March/April 1998, pp. 59–65, 96.
43. John Hockenberry. *I.D. Magazine*, March/April 1998, pp. 59–65, 96.
44. Richard Corliss. "Beauty and the Beast," *Time*, April 20, 1998, pp. 66–70.
45. Kathryn Harris. "The Loneliest Man in the Kingdom," *Los Angeles Times*, March 26, 1995.

BIBLIOGRAPHY

Albrecht, Karl, and Ron Zemke. *Service America*. New York, Warner Books, 1985.

Allen, Thomas J. *Managing the Flow of Technology*. Cambridge, MA, The MIT Press, 1977.

Byrman, Alan. *Disney and His Worlds*. London, Routledge, 1995.

Connellan, Tom. *Inside the Magic Kingdom*. Austin, TX, Bard Press, 1996.

Cotter, Bill. *The Wonderful World of Disney Television*. New York, Disney Enterprises, Hyperion, 1997.

Disney, Walt. *Walt Disney: Famous Quotes*. Lake Buena Vista, FL, The Walt Disney Company, 1994.

Dunlop, Beth. *Building a Dream: The Art of Disney Architecture*. New York, Harry N. Abrams, Inc., 1996.

Eliot, Marc. *Walt Disney: Hollywood's Dark Prince*. New York, HarperCollins, 1993.

France, Van Arsdale. *Window on Main Street: 35 Years of Creating Happiness at Disneyland Park*. Nashua, NH, Laugher Publications, Inc./Stabur Press, Inc., 1991.

Ghoshal, Sumantra, and Christopher A. Bartlett. *The Individualized Corporation: A Fundamentally New Approach to Management*. New York, Harper Business, 1997.

Grant, John. *Encyclopedia of Walt Disney's Animated Characters from Mickey Mouse to Aladdin*. New York, The Walt Disney Company, Hyperion, 1993.

Greene, Katherine, and Richard Greene. *The Man Behind the Magic*. New York, Penguin Books, 1991.

Grover, Ron. *The Disney Touch: How a Daring Management Team Revived an Entertainment Empire*. Homewood, IL, BusinessOne Irwin, 1991.

Hollis, Richard, and Brian Sibley. *Walt Disney's Snow White and the Seven Dwarfs & The Making of The Classic Film*. New York, The Walt Disney Company, Hyperion, 1994.

Imagineers. *Walt Disney Imagineering: A Behind the Dreams Look at Making the Magic Real*. New York, Disney Enterprises, Inc., Hyperion, 1996.

Kurth, Jeff. *Since the World Began—Walt Disney World: The First 25 Years*. New York, Disney Enterprises, Inc., Hyperion, 1996.

Labovitz, George, and Victor Rosansky. *The Power of Alignment: How Great Companies Stay Centered and Accomplich Extraordinary Things.* New York, John Wiley & Sons, Inc., 1997.

LeBoeuf, Michael. *Imagineering.* New York, Berkley Books, 1980.

Maltin, Leonard. *The Disney Films,* 3d ed. New York, JessieFilm Ltd., Hyperion, 1995.

Marling, Karal Ann (ed.). *Designing Disney's Theme Parks: The Architecture of Reassurance.* Montreal, Canada, Centre Canadien d'Architecture, Flammarion, Paris, New York. 1997.

Mosley, Leonard. *Disney's World.* Lanham, MD, Scarborough House, 1990.

Neary, Kevin, and Dave Smith. *The Ultimate Disney Trivia Book.* New York, Hyperion, 1992.

Neary, Kevin, and Dave Smith. *The Ultimate Disney Trivia Book* 2. New York, Hyperion, 1994.

Neary, Kevin, and Dave Smith. *The Ultimate Disney Trivia Book* 3. New York, Hyperion, 1997.

Santoli, Lorraine. *The Official Mickey Mouse Club.* New York, Hyperion, 1995.

Schroeder, Russell (ed.). *Walt Disney: His Life in Pictures.* New York, Disney Press, 1996.

Schroeder, Russell. *Walt Disney's Mickey Mouse: My Life in Pictures.* New York, Disney Enterprises, Inc., Hyperion, 1997.

Sheridan, Bruce. *Policy Deployment.* Milwaukee, WI, ASQC Quality Press, 1993.

Smith, Dave. *Disney A to Z.* New York, Disney Enterprises, Inc., Hyperion, 1996.

Solomon, Charles. *The Disney That Never Was.* New York, The Walt Disney Company, Inc., 1995.

Spector, Robert, and Patrick D. McCarthy. *The Nordstrom Way.* New York. John Wiley & Sons, Inc., 1995.

Thomas, Bob. *Disney's Art of Animation: From Mickey Mouse to Beauty and the Beast.* New York, Welcome Enterprises, Inc., Hyperion, 1991.

Thomas, Bob. *Walt Disney: An American Original.* New York, Pocket Books, 1976.

Vance, Mike, and Diane Deacon. *Think Out of the Box.* Franklin Lakes, NJ, The Career Press, 1995.

Vance, Mike. *A Kitchen for the Mind* (audiotape series). Cleveland, OH, Intellectual Equities, Inc.

Vance, Mike. *Creative Thinking* (audiotape series). Chicago, IL, Nightingale Conant Corporation.

Vance, Mike. *Entrepreneurial Thinking* (audiotape series). Niles, IL, Mike Vance/Intellectual Equities, Inc./Nightingale Conant Corporation.

Vance, Mike. *Motivational Thinking* (audiotape series). Cleveland, OH. Intellectual Equities, Inc.

Walt Disney World Resort: A Magical Year-by-Year Journey. New York, Disney Enterprises, Inc., Hyperion, 1998.

Walton, Mary. *The Deming Management Method.* New York, The Putnam Publishing Group, 1986.

Zemke, Ron. *The Service Edge.* New York, NAL Books, 1989.

INDEX

ABOUT THE AUTHORS

Together, BILL CAPODAGLI and LYNN JACKSON represent nearly fifty years of consulting, business, and corporate research expertise. They founded Capodagli Jackson Consulting in 1993, and work with companies to implement *The Disney Way* principles. Since the original release of *The Disney Way* in 1999, Bill and Lynn have been in constant demand with their exciting, hands-on "Creating the Magic with Dream, Believe, Dare, Do" seminars. Bill has become one of the most popular keynote speakers for both national and international conferences. *The Disney Way* is published in eight languages and has earned the reputation as one of the most enduring leadership manifestos of our time.

Capodagli Jackson is based in Indianapolis. For information on seminars and keynotes, please call 800-238-9958 or email dreamovations@aol.com.